Peter Buchs & Thomas Honegger
(editors)

NEWS FROM THE SHIRE AND BEYOND – STUDIES ON TOLKIEN
Second Edition

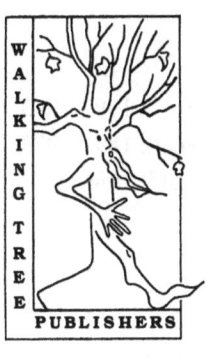

2004

Cormarë Series

No 1

Series Editors
Peter Buchs • Thomas Honegger • Andrew Moglestue

Edited by
Peter Buchs • Thomas Honegger

Library of Congress Cataloging-in-Publication Data

Buchs, Peter and Thomas Honegger (eds.)
  News from the Shire and Beyond – Studies on Tolkien
  2nd edition.
  ISBN 3-9521424-5-X

Subject headings:
Tolkien, J. R. R. (John Ronald Reuel), 1892-1973 – Criticism and interpretation
Tolkien, J. R. R. (John Ronald Reuel), 1892-1973 – Language
Fantasy fiction, English - History and criticism
Middle-earth (Imaginary place)
Literature, Comparative.

All rights reserved. No portion of this book may be reproduced, by any process or technique, without the express written consent of the publisher.

First published in 1997. 2nd edition in 2004.
Walking Tree Publishers, Zurich and Berne 2004.
Printed by Lightning Source in the United Kingdom and the United States.

To our beloved ones
-
Auria
Faolchù Fionn
and one
- at the time of the first publication -
as yet unborn

Acknowledgments

We wish to express our deepest gratitude to all those who have contributed in one way or another to this volume.

In particular, we would like to thank Andrew Moglestue, who proofread all papers and who helped to get our 'Swenglish' into an acceptable form.

Furthermore, our sincere thanks are also due to Auria Buchs-Alves who made the publication of the maps for Peter Buchs' and Nils-Lennart Johannesson's articles possible.

Moreover, we wish to thank The Swiss Tolkien Society for the permission to publish these papers. The majority of them were given at the Cormarë Conference in September 1996.

Thanks are also due to Walking Tree Publishers for financing this project.

Finally, a word of praise and appreciation must go to Sabina Müller, whose drawing was used for the logo of Walking Tree Publishers.

Spring 2004
Peter Buchs and Thomas Honegger

TABLE OF CONTENTS

Preface to the Second Edition *Peter Buchs and Thomas Honegger*	1
Tolkien Studies: News from the Shire and Beyond Indeed *Peter Buchs and Thomas Honegger*	3
The Speech of the Individual and of the Community in *The Lord of the Rings* *Nils-Lennart Johannesson*	13
From Bag End to Lórien: the Creation of a Literary World *Thomas Honegger*	59
Middle Earth: The Collectible Card Game – Powerplay in the World of Tolkien *Patrick Näf*	83
Middle-earth: the Wizards – the Representation of Tolkien's World in the Game *Peter Buchs*	103
Notes on the Contributors	162

Preface to the Second Edition

Early in 1997 a couple of members of the Swiss Tolkien Society founded Walking Tree Publishers in order to make possible the publication of the papers of the Cormarë Conference, which the Swiss Tolkien Society had held in Seelisberg, Switzerland in September 1996. At the time the venture was regarded as highly risky and it was not quite sure whether the invested money could ever be recovered. The co-founders and co-owners of Walking Tree Publishers were, however, convinced of the merits of the project and decided to go ahead regardless of the financial risk. During the preliminary discussions the co-owners of Walking Tree Publishers already started to think big and decided that the proceeds of the sale of the publication would rather be reinvested in new projects than be paid back to the original investors. Walking Tree Publishers were to be run as a non-profit organization.

When *News from the Shire and Beyond – Studies on Tolkien* finally was put on the market, it soon became clear that it would be a success and that the modest 50 copies that had been printed would not last long. In autumn 1998 it was sold out and the sales proceeds allowed other projects to be realized. Over the last 6 years no less than three collections of essays, two full studies and two literary sub-creations set in Middle-earth were published by Walking Tree Publishers in ever-increasing numbers of copies and we are going stronger than ever.

With the high upfront costs of conventional printing a reprint of *News from the Shire and Beyond - Studies on Tolkien*, however, remained unthinkable for a very long time. Only with new IT-technologies and print on demand services made generally available, Walking Tree Publishers could finally think about putting the collection of essays on the market again. This new edition of *News from the Shire and Beyond - Studies on Tolkien* consists of five out of the six items of the original edition, one author having preferred to withdraw his contribution. The various essays are basically reprinted in the form in which they were first published in 1997 and have not been systematically updated to include either new research results or present academic or popular trends – notwithstanding minor reworking of individual passages. We are convinced that the various ideas that were circulated back in 1997 are still of some considerable interest to the Tolkien reader today and he (or she as it may be) should not remain deprived of them.

Spring 2004
Peter Buchs and Thomas Honegger

Tolkien Studies:
News from the Shire and Beyond Indeed

PETER BUCHS AND THOMAS HONEGGER

In 1968 Neil D. Isaacs and Rose Zimbardo launched their first 'effort to save Tolkien from the faddists and the button makers', which they kept up by the publication of another volume of critical essays in 1979. Today, nearly 30 years after this early call to arms, Tolkien is no longer in need of being 'saved' from anyone – be it the faddists, button makers or even the academics. True, to the general public he still is primarily the author of *The Hobbit* and *The Lord of the Rings*, the creator of those cute little fellas with fur on their feet. And it is the 'popular' aspect of his work that has been taken up and exploited by the 'faddists and button makers' against whom Isaacs and Zimbardo's academic wrath was directed. However, Tolkien has proven quite resistant to these afflictions which could easily have been the doom of a lesser work. Although a recent poll in Great Britain had *The Lord of the Rings* pronounced the most important work of 20th century fiction[1], it has been spared from the worst excesses of full-scale merchandising, in part thanks to a fairly restrictive copyright policy of the Tolkien Trust. At the same time, Tolkien has slowly outgrown his popular categorization as 'fantasy'. If bookstore classifications reflect the estimation of the general public, then Tolkien is definitively 'on his way out' of the SF & Fantasy department proper. Whether he will end up in the 'general fiction' department or not remains to be seen. At the moment, however, he seems to hover in a kind of classificatory limbo. Most bigger bookstores in Britain have solved this problem by alloting Tolkien and books on Tolkien and Middle-earth a shelf or even a section of their own. This is not so much the merit of any attempt on the side of literary critics, as rather due to the immense popularity which all of Tolkien's works, deservedly or not, enjoy. This popularity has also led publishers to reprint not only all of Tolkien's

---

1 Tolkien's epos was selected as the most important book published in the 20th century in a survey of more than 25'000 book-shop customers which was conducted in 1997.

earlier works of fiction, but likewise to undertake the publication of material which may be of interest to the Tolkien scholar, but which is hardly attractive to the general reader.[2]

So far we have mostly been concerned with Tolkien as seen by the 'general public', i.e. by those readers who know him as the author of *The Hobbit* and *The Lord of the Rings*, and maybe *The Silmarillion*, but who have never developed a more than temporary interest in his work (and life). Thus, in a next step, we will engage in a discussion of those people who have shown a more serious commitment to Tolkien and his work: the 'amateurs'[3] and the 'professionals'.

The division in 'amateurs' and 'professionals' has purely pragmatic character, and the two terms are not mutually exclusive. From the point of view of classification, it would be much more satisfactory, if we were able to draw a clear line between 'amateur' publications, implying a value judgment on both form (fanzines) and content, in the unflattering sense of the word, and those that lay claim to professional status. Unfortunately, things are not that clear-cut since, as we all know, 'all that is gold does not glitter,' nor is all that glitters gold. Many a humbly photocopied fanzine offers articles that put professional publications to shame. The criterion for the division into 'amateur' and 'professional' is thus not quality, but form.

The amateurs of Tolkien studies very often meet with other Tolkien fans in literary societies dedicated to the study of the life and works of Prof. J.R.R. Tolkien. The most prominent of these societies are the Tolkien Society (GB) and the Mythopoeic Society (USA), but such societies are also found in the Netherlands, Denmark, Norway, Sweden, Finland, Poland, Italy, Switzerland and many more countries. Most of these societies offer the more interested reader publications and literary conferences in which various aspects of Tolkien's life and works are discussed at great length. These

---

2 The whole of the 'History of Middle-earth'-series belongs to this material.

3 We prefer the neutral term 'amateurs' to Isaacs and Zimbardo's derogatory 'faddists', as the persons in question, besides having often joined in the fun of Tolkien fandom, have also largely contributed to Tolkien studies.

contributions can vary from the raw sketch of a new interpretation of a given text sample taking a couple of pages in a Tolkien fanzine to an elaborate linguistic or literary essay presented at an international conference. So far, amateur scholars have used two major approaches in their studies as was first pointed out by Patricia Reynolds and John Ellison in 1994.[4] The first one, Tolkien Studies, looks at J.R.R. Tolkien as a creative artist. It is interested in his literary sources, in his technique as a writer and his reception by critics, the general public and other authors. The second approach, Middle-earth Studies, on the contrary, treats Middle-earth as a 'real' world with peoples, languages, a geography and a history of its own. This second approach is not so much interested in the author, but in his creation. Middle-earth Studies, in their vast majority, regard J.R.R. Tolkien's works as accounts of historical events which took place in Middle-earth and aim at finding out the truth about them. The Middle-earth Studies approach has, however, also given rise to an artistic derivative. Based on Tolkien's very own concept of sub-creation Tolkien amateurs find themselves writing tales and poetry and drawing artwork set in Middle-earth.

In the following discussion of 'professional' publications, we won't consider radio plays, movies, comics and other media, but limit ourselves to books. Yet, even with this self-imposed limitation, we find ourselves still confronted with a plethora of printed matter on the topic. The discussion will therefore be of summary nature. Also, the bibliographical references are fragmentary, though hopefully illustrative, since no attempt at completeness has been made.[5]

The first serious attempts at book-length studies of Tolkien's work seem to have their roots in his spectacular popularity in the sixties. Thus, in 1969, J.S. Ryan thought it appropriate to choose the question *Tolkien: Cult or Culture?* as title for his study, and the seventies continued the debate about

---

4 Reynolds and Ellison in *Mallorn* No. 31 (1994:5-6).
5 Principal bibliographical works to be consulted are West (1991) and Hammond (1993). Continuing bibliographical material may be found on the web-page of the Tolkien Society (GB).

Tolkien's status. Yet, at the same time Tolkien's work became not only the centre of literary discussion, but also the subject of more general literary studies. Scholars like Reilly (1971), Urang (1971) and Sale (1973) no longer question his status as 'literature', but include his work, along with that of other authors, in their analyses of aspects of literature.[6] Of similar importance for the emancipation of Tolkien studies and the acceptance of his fictional work in academic circles are dissertations.[7] The times when a thesis-project was rejected on the grounds that the department did not want a study on 'little people with hair on their feet' are hopefully a thing of the past. Most dissertations start from a general literary problem and use Tolkien and other authors to test their approach. They are thus not primarily concerned with problems and questions typical of Tolkien. Those questions have, however, been dealt with in a number of studies that either treat Tolkien's work in its entirety or select certain aspects for discussion.[8] Not surprisingly, the study of the mythological and symbolical is especially prominent in this field.[9] Publications that analyse Tolkien's work from a psychoanalytical point of view seem to be equally popular.[10] The last two categories in our list of studies that have helped to consolidate Tolkien's position in literature both belong to the world of education. Their respective target groups, however, differ considerably. The first category of books comprises 'notes' or 'study aids', aimed at High School/Grammar School students, undergraduates or teachers that have to come to terms with

---

6   This approach has been continued by authors like Grant (1979), Achterberg (1982), Little (1984), Rossi (1984), Schütze (1984) and Knight (1990).

7   Dissertations that were later on published as books are Petzold (1980), Achterberg (1982), Rossi (1984), and Schütze (1986).

8   Studies of more general nature are those by Kocher (1972), Mathews (1978), Petzold (1980), Shippey (1982/1992), Rosebury (1992), and Stevens and Stevens (1993). Proceedings of conferences and workshops on Tolkien, such as P. Reynolds and GoodKnight (1995) and various workshop proceedings by the Tolkien Society (GB), illuminate individual aspects of his work.

9   The discussion of myth, symbol and religion has been the subject of various books. Thus, Miesel (1973), Noel (1977), Nitzsche (1979), Petty (1979), Harvey (1981), Uyldert (1988) and Day (1994) treat one or several of these topics.

10 See Spice (1976), O'Neill (1980), and Green (1995).

Tolkien's fiction as part of their curricula.[11] The second category consists of publications that focus on the otherwise neglected scholarly aspects of his work and thus try to reclaim him, at least partially, for the academic community.[12] Biographies, be they about Tolkien himself[13] or about his intellectual environment[14], round off the picture.

Most types of 'professional' publications discussed so far have not been specifically Tolkienian – except, of course, for their subject matter. Biographies, literary interpretations, study aids etc. are common genres in the field of literary studies. There remain, as a result, those publications that are in some way or other quite specifically, though admittedly not exclusively, Tolkienian. The first category has its origin in the encyclopaedic tradition. The flora and fauna, the races, peoples, languages as well as the geography of Middle-earth have been described in a number of publications.[15] The quality and scope of this descriptive approach is quite unique in the context of literary fiction and testifies to the impact of Tolkien's sub-creative powers. The second category is similarly indebted to the concept of sub-creation. It comprises stories and other works of fiction by professional writers which are situated in Tolkien's world and 'continue' Tolkien's process of sub-creation.[16]

Where within this landscape, then, is the place of the present volume? From a purely formalistic point of view, it must be classified together with the

---

11 We included Ready (1971), Hardy (1977), Ridden (1981), Foster (1981) and Pienciak (1986) in this category.

12 Examples are Salu and Farrell (1979) and Gray (1992).

13 Carpenter (1977) and Grotta (1979).

14 Carpenter (1978).

15 Day (1979), Day (1991), and Day (1993) offer such encyclopaedic treatments. Information on the languages of Middle-earth in general can be found in Noel (1980), and on Elvish in particular in Kloczko (1995). The atlas by Fonstad (1992) gives a uniquely rich and accurate description of Middle-earth throughout the ages. Less comprehensive, yet a valuable guide to the travels in *The Lord of the Rings*, is Strachey (1981). Handbooks (Tyler 1979 and Duriez 1992) and the thesaurus by Blackwelder (1990) should be mentioned in this context, too.

16 This category mirrors the pieces of imaginative fiction found in fanzines. Greenberg (1992) is the only book-publication known to us that falls into this class.

'conference proceedings'. The contributions collected in this book were all presented on the occasion of the tenth anniversary of the Swiss Tolkien Society 'Eredain' in 1996. They were either given as guest lecture at the English Department of the University of Zurich (Johannesson) or as part of the Cormarë conference at Seelisberg (Honegger, Näf, and Buchs). The first two studies (Johannesson and Honegger) deal with 'traditional' Tolkien subject matter. Thus, Johannesson's paper is a linguistic analysis of the non-standard English forms and constructions used by Tolkien to characterize speaker groups and individual speakers in *The Lord of the Rings*. Were it not for his choice of data, his study might as well be published in any scholarly journal on linguistics. Honegger, then, discusses the importance of places and space in the creation of Tolkien's literary universe. Although his study is concerned with a central and thus, in its prominence, specifically Tolkienian aspect, the approach is more general and Tolkien is used as an especially suitable example. The following two contributions (Näf and Buchs) expand the horizon and, in their discussion of the recent collectable card phenomenon, cross the border into fairly uncharted territory. Näf introduces the reader to the Tolkien-based collectable card game *Middle-earth: the Wizards*. In his study he shows the set-up of the game, exemplifies its rules and assesses the artwork on its cards. Buchs, on the contrary, focuses on the quality with which Middle-earth reality, as testified by Tolkien's writings, is translated into *Middle-earth: the Wizards*. His study ends in a short outlook on the potential development of collectable card games based on Tolkien's writings.

We hope that these specimen of Tolkien scholarship offer, in the Horatian sense, both entertainment and edification to the reader and add to his or her enjoyment and appreciation of Tolkien's work.

REFERENCES

ACHTERBERG, Bernhard. 1982. *Entfaltung eines Konzeptes von Verantwortung in Auseinandersetzung mit den Werken von Tolkien und Castaneda*. Dissertation (GS Kassel).

BLACKWELDER, Richard E. 1990. *A Tolkien Thesaurus*. New York: Garland.

CARPENTER, Humphrey. 1977. *Tolkien: A Biography*. London: Allen and Unwin.

– – –. 1978. *The Inklings: C.S. Lewis, J.R.R. Tolkien, Charles Williams, and Their Friends*. London: Allen and Unwin.

DAY, David. 1979. *A Tolkien Bestiary*. London: Mitchell Beazley.

– – –. 1991. *Tolkien: The Illustrated Encyclopedia*. London: Mitchell Beazley.

– – –. 1993. *The Tolkien Companion*. London: Mandarin.

– – –. 1994. *Tolkien's Ring*. London: HarperCollins.

DURIEZ, Colin. 1992. *The J.R.R. Tolkien Handbook*. Grand Rapids, Michigan: Baker Book House.

FONSTAD, Karen Wynn. 1992. *The Atlas of Middle-Earth*. Second, revised edition. First edition 1981. London: HarperCollins.

FOSTER, Robert. 1981. *Teacher's Guide to The Hobbit*. New York: Ballantine Books.

GRANT, Patrick. 1979. *Six Modern Authors and Problems of Belief*. London: Macmillan.

GRAY, Rosemary. 1992. *A Tribute to J.R.R. Tolkien*. Pretoria: Unisa.

GREEN, William H. 1995. *The Hobbit: A Journey into Maturity*. New York: Twayne Publishers.

GREENBERG, Martin H. (ed.). 1992. *After the King: Stories in Honor of J.R.R. Tolkien*. New York: Doherty.

GROTTA, Daniel. 1978. *The Biography of J.R.R. Tolkien: Architect of Middle-earth*. Philadelphia: Running Press.

HAMMOND, Wayne G., with the assistance of Douglas A. Anderson. 1993. *J.R.R. Tolkien: A Descriptive Bibliography*. Winchester: St. Paul's Bibliographies.

HARDY, Gene B. 1977. *Tolkien's The Lord of the Rings and The Hobbit: Notes*. Lincoln, Nebraska: Cliff Notes, Inc.

HARVEY, David. 1981. *The Song of Middle-earth: J.R.R. Tolkien's Themes, Symbols and Myths*. London: Allen and Unwin.

ISAACS, Neil D. and Rose A. ZIMBARDO (eds.). 1968. *Tolkien and the Critics: Essays on J.R.R. Tolkien's The Lord of the Rings*. Notre Dame and London: University of Notre Dame Press.

– – –. 1979. *Tolkien: New Critical Perspectives*. Lexington, Kentucky: The University Press of Kentucky.

KLOCZKO, Edouard. 1995. *Dictionnaire des langues elfiques*. Volume 1. Toulon: Tamise.

KNIGHT, Gareth. 1990. *The Magical World of the Inklings: J.R.R. Tolkien, C.S. Lewis, Charles Williams, Owen Barfield*. Longmead: Element Books.

KOCHER, Paul H. 1972. *The Master of Middle-earth: The Fiction of J.R.R. Tolkien*. Boston: Houghton Mifflin.

LITTLE, Edmund. 1984. *The Fantasts: J.R.R. Tolkien, Lewis Carroll, Mervyn Peake, Nikolay Gogol and Kenneth Grahame*. Avebury: Amersham.

MATHEWS, Richard. 1978. *Lightning from a Clear Sky: Tolkien, the Trilogy, and the Silmarillion*. San Bernardino: Borgo Press.

MIESEL, Sandra. 1973. *Myth, Symbol and Religion in The Lord of the Rings*. Baltimore, Maryland: T-K Graphics.

NOEL, Ruth S. 1977. *The Mythology of Middle-Earth*. Boston: Houghton Mifflin.

– – –. 1980. *The Languages of Tolkien's Middle-earth*. First published 1974. Boston: Houghton Mifflin.

NITZSCHE, Jane Chance. 1979. *Tolkien's Art: 'A Mythology for England'*. London: Macmillan.

O'NEILL, Timothy R. 1979. *The Individuated Hobbit: Jung, Tolkien and the Archetypes of Middle-earth*. Boston: Houghton Mifflin.

PETTY, Anne C. 1979. *One Ring to Bind Them All: Tolkien's Mythology*. University of Alabama Press.

PETZOLD, Dieter. 1980. *J.R.R. Tolkien: Fantasy Literatur als Wunscherfüllung und Weltdeutung*. Heidelberg: Carl Winter Universitätsverlag.

PIENCIAK, Anne M. 1986. *J.R.R. Tolkien's The Hobbit and The Lord of the Rings*. Barron's Book Notes, Barron's Educational Series.

READY, William. 1971. *The Lord of the Rings, The Hobbit: Notes*. Coles Notes. Toronto: Coles Publishing Co.

REILLY, Robert J. 1971. *Romantic Religion: A Study of Barfield, Lewis, Williams, and Tolkien*. Athens, Georgia: University of Georgia Press.

REYNOLDS, Patricia and John ELLISON. 1994. »Editorial.« In: *Mallorn* 31. Edited by Reynolds, Patricia and John Ellison. Milton Keynes: The Tolkien Society, 5-6.

REYNOLDS, Patricia and Glen H. GOODKNIGHT (eds.). 1995. *Proceedings of the J.R.R. Tolkien Centenary Conference*. Mythlore 80 / Mallorn 30. Milton Keynes and Altadena: The Tolkien Society and The Mythopoeic Society.

REYNOLDS, Trevor (ed.). 1992. *The First and Second Ages: The 5th Tolkien Society Workshop*. London: The Tolkien Society.

RIDDEN, Geoffrey. 1981. *J.R.R. Tolkien: The Hobbit*. York Notes. Beirut: York Press.

ROSEBURY, Brian. 1992. *Tolkien: A Critical Assessment*. London: Macmillan/St. Martin's Press.

ROSSI, Lee D. 1984. *The Politics of Fantasy: C.S. Lewis and J.R.R. Tolkien*. Ann Arbor: UMI Research Press.

RYAN, J.S. 1969. *Tolkien: Cult or Culture?* Armindale, N.S.W.: University of New England.

SALE, Roger. 1973. *Modern Heroism: Essays on D.H. Lawrence, William Empson, and J.R.R. Tolkien*. Berkeley and Los Angeles: University of California Press.

SALU, Mary and Robert T. FARRELL (eds.) 1979. *J.R.R. Tolkien, Scholar and Storyteller: Essays in Memoriam*. Ithaca and London: Cornell University Press.

SCHÜTZE, Marli. 1986. *Neue Wege nach Narnia und Mittelerde: Handlungskonstituenten in der Fantasy-Literatur von C.S. Lewis und J.R.R. Tolkien*. Frankfurt am Main and Bern: Peter Lang.

SHIPPEY, Tom A. 1982. *The Road to Middle-earth*. London: Allen and Unwin. Second, revised edition 1992. London: Grafton.

SPICE, Wilma Helen. 1976. *A Jungian View of Tolkien's 'Gandalf': An Investigation of Enabling and Exploitative Power in Counseling and Psychotherapy from the Viewpoint of Analytical Psychology*. Ann Arbor, Michigan: Dissertation, University of Pittsburg.

STEVENS, Carol D. and David STEVENS. 1993. *J.R.R. Tolkien: The Art of the Myth-maker*. San Bernardino: Borgo Press.

STRACHEY, Barbara. 1981. *Journeys of Frodo: An Atlas of J.R.R. Tolkien's The Lord of the Rings*. Unwin Paperbacks. London: Allen and Unwin.

TYLER, J.E.A. 1979. *The New Tolkien Companion*. London: Macmillan.

URANG, Gunnar. 1971. *Shadows of Heaven: Religion and Fantasy in the Writings of C.S. Lewis, Charles Williams, and J.R.R. Tolkien*. London: SCM Press.

UYLDERT, Mellie. 1988. *Die Entdeckung von Mittelerde: Symbolik von Tolkiens 'Der Herr der Ringe'*. Munich: Hugendubel.

WEST, Richard C. 1991. *Tolkien Criticism: An Annotated Checklist*. The Serif Series 39. The Kent State University Press.

The Speech of the Individual and of the Community in *The Lord of the Rings*[1]

NILS-LENNART JOHANNESSON

Summary

Non-standard English forms and constructions, drawn from the rural dialects of Oxfordshire and Warwickshire, function as very versatile tools in the characterization of speaker groups and individual speakers in *The Lord of the Rings*. In the speech of working-class Shire hobbits and Breelanders, the use of these non-standard features suggests group solidarity and linguistic insecurity as well as regional dialect differences within the Shire and accommodation to other people's speech.

> "Don't the great tales never end?"
> (Sam Gamgee)

> "Don't adventures ever have an end?"
> (Bilbo Baggins)

1 INTRODUCTION

1.1 Background

The Shire is reported to have measured forty leagues (120 miles) from east to west and fifty leagues (150 miles) from north to south (LotR Prol. I:16[2]), an area comparable to England south of the Wash (less Cornwall). It was, in

---

[1] Three earlier versions of this paper (under as many different titles) saw the light of day between 1983 and 1993. I owe a great debt of gratitude to the following persons for various kinds of input and criticism over the years: Stanley Ellis, the late Ossi Ihalainen, Gunnel Melchers, Clive Upton and, last but not least, Beregond, Anders Stenström. The responsibility for views, data and interpretations presented here is, needless to say, my own. I am grateful to the Swiss Tolkien Society for giving me this opportunity to bring out a revised and corrected version of this paper (although, alas, it has not been possible to update the list of references).

[2] All references to *The Lord of the Rings* (henceforth LotR) will have the form book number, chapter number and paragraph number. In the case of the Prologue, references will have the form section name and paragraph number (separated by a colon). Reference to paragraph in this manner makes it possible to identify the relevant passage irrespective of which edition is being used.

other words, large enough to accommodate a number of dialect areas. The Shire was, furthermore, a country among whose inhabitants at the end of the Third Age different socioeconomic classes can be recognized: agricultural workers and craftsmen of various kinds, landowners, civil servants (messengers, shirriffs, bounders), commercial entrepreneurs at all levels (ranging from butchers, grocers and inn-keepers to the emerging big-time capitalist Lotho Sackville-Baggins), as well as rentiers and members of a hereditary aristocracy. The educational background of the hobbits apparently varied considerably (illiteracy does not seem to have been uncommon; cf. LotR 4 IV:27). As can be expected in a flourishing society, we also find hobbits of all ages and both sexes in the Shire.[3]

The Shire was, in short, precisely the kind of society in which we can expect to encounter regionally and socially determined variation in the speech of its inhabitants: the hobbits in one village can be expected to speak differently from those in the next village, and the upper classes will presumably speak differently from the farmhands.

In an everyday speech situation, a speaker may produce an utterance with the intention of conveying certain information to a hearer. At the same time, however, the same utterance may convey additional information to a perceptive hearer, information which the speaker never intended to convey. The utterance in question may indicate to the hearer that the speaker comes from the Glasgow area, is a member of the working class, is angry, and is slightly drunk. Another way of describing this situation is to say that various features in the speaker's speech may function as **indices**: they **indicate** that the speaker belongs to a particular group (in which case we may distinguish between **social**, **regional**, and **age-related group-identifying indices**), or they indicate some aspect of the speaker's psychological or physical state (in which case we say that the linguistic features are **symptoms** of that state).

---

3   For a more detailed account of the socioeconomic situation in the Shire the reader is referred to Crawford 1985:1-9.

It is the purpose of this paper to examine one aspect of Tolkien's handling of the English language in LotR, namely his use of linguistic forms and constructions, in particular non-standard ones, to characterize individual speakers and groups of speakers, primarily hobbits, in LotR (or, to put it differently, to investigate the indexical function of those forms and constructions). Some of these forms and constructions may well pass unnoticed by some readers, but to the extent they are noticed they will help create the picture of a speech community with considerable internal variation.

1.2 Linguistic and non-linguistic variables

The linguistic data for this study have been gathered from all the prose passages spoken by hobbits and other characters in LotR; for the purposes of this paper, any passage which is not typographically marked as verse has been regarded as prose. Both phonological and syntactic variables will, as far as possible, be taken into account. However, since the linguistic material is available only in standard English orthography, no detailed phonological study can be undertaken. The discussion of phonological variation will be restricted to deletion of initial and final consonants, as represented by the use of the forms *'ee*, *'em*, and *o'*. By contrast, the material is much richer in different types of syntactic variation. Seven different syntactic variables have been selected for discussion in the present paper, namely

i   sentence negation,
ii   subject-verb agreement,
iii   auxiliary contraction,
iv   progressive verb forms,
v   perfect tense forms,
vi   relative pronouns,
vii   constructions with *ought to*.

These variables all have variants which function as markers of social class (social group-identifying indices) among hobbits; in addition, some of them have variants which can be interpreted as having other functions as well.

The social classification of hobbits will by necessity have to be rather crude, since the available linguistic material from most hobbits (apart from Frodo, Sam, Merry and Pippin) is so scanty. A primary distinction between HOBBITS and NON-HOBBITS (dwarves, elves, ents, men, orcs, etc.) will be made. Among the hobbits, two social classes will be recognized: a LEISURE CLASS (LC), whose members do not have to work for a living, comprising gentlehobbits of independent means (Bilbo, Frodo) as well as sons of wealthy landowners (Merry, Pippin), and a WORKING CLASS (WC), comprising farmers, gardeners, millers, ropers, shirriffs, etc. Apart from this social variable, regional and age-related variability will also be considered.

1.3 Non-standard forms

Strictly speaking, any linguistic form which can be given a contrastive function can be used to illustrate social class distinctions in speech, but the message comes across much more clearly to the reader if the forms used are known to have a similar function in the primary world. It can therefore be instructive to consider briefly what non-standard English forms Tolkien used to represent the speech of WC hobbits.

In a letter to Allen and Unwin 1955 Tolkien stated that the Shire "is in fact more or less a Warwickshire village about the period of the Diamond Jubilee"[4] (Carpenter 1981:230, letter no. 178). Kilby (1976:51) describes how Tolkien, during a car ride through Oxfordshire, pointed to some hills which he said "were just right for hobbit territory". These two statements should be seen as complementary rather than contradictory: the two neighbouring counties of Warwickshire and Oxfordshire provided the geographical raw material that Tolkien transformed into the scenery of the Shire.

---

4 *Diamond Jubilee*: the celebration of the sixtieth year of Queen Victoria's reign in 1897.

Although nothing is said in the passages quoted above about language matters, it would seem natural to expect Tolkien to have used the dialect of Warwickshire/Oxfordshire as the linguistic raw material from which he created the English representation of 'Shiretalk', the vernacular of the Shire hobbits. A close study of the non-standard English forms used in hobbit dialogue confirms that this is indeed the case: with one exception, as we shall see, all the dialectal forms used to represent Shiretalk are such as have been recorded in the speech of dialect speakers from Warwickshire/Oxfordshire.

An invaluable source of information during the preparation of this paper was the published material of the Survey of English Dialects, a large-scale investigation of traditional rural dialects in England. What makes the Survey material specially valuable for the purposes of this paper is the fact that, although the fieldwork was mostly carried out in the 1950's and early 60's, all the informants were born in the 1870's and 80's. Thus their speech habits had just been formed at the time of the Diamond Jubilee, and the forms and constructions they used should correspond well to the rural speech that Tolkien will have heard in the Warwickshire of his boyhood. The informant responses are available in undigested form in the so-called *Basic Material*, a set of volumes covering the four Survey regions (the North, the East Midlands, the West Midlands, and the South). The dialect data for this paper have primarily been collected from the West Midland volumes of the *Basic Material* (Orton and Barry 1969-71, henceforth BM). In addition I have consulted *The Linguistic Atlas of England* (Orton et al. 1978, henceforth *LAE*), a cartographic (interpretative) representation of Survey data.

A comparison between the hobbit dialogue in LotR and the Survey material shows that Tolkien's use of dialectal Warwickshire/Oxfordshire forms was selective rather than wholesale. His guiding principle seems to have been to avoid too markedly localized forms and instead to rely on forms with a fairly wide distribution in English dialects, forms which could be slipped in unobtrusively in the speech of Shire hobbits. For example, the widely used form *lass* is used to refer to hobbit girls (in dialogue as well as in narrative text) rather than the more typical West Midland form *wench*[5].

Although the forms used have a wide distribution in English dialects, the joint occurrence of certain items is highly indicative of Warwickshire/Oxfordshire dialect forms: the relative pronoun *as* is chiefly a West Midland form (*LAE* map S5), *(we/they) be* ('(we/they) are') is chiefly a South-Western form (*LAE* maps M8, M19), and *ain't* ('am/are/is not') is chiefly an East Midland and South-Eastern form (*LAE* maps M13-15). The only area in England where the three items occur together, according to the maps in *LAE*, would be Buckinghamshire, which would not seem to agree particularly well with the Warwickshire/Oxfordshire hypothesis. However, this Buckinghamshire localization is based on the assumption that *ain't* should be given its most widespread pronunciation, namely [eɪnt]. The most common pronunciation in Warwickshire and Oxfordshire, however, is [ent]: it is used by three out of four informants in Warwickshire and by six out of seven informants in Oxfordshire (*BM* 1053). Given this pronunciation of *ain't*, the three items are found to co-occur in Oxfordshire and southern Warwick-shire, as shown in Figure 1.

The pronunciation of *ain't* as [ent] can furthermore be seen as meaningful in two contexts in LotR, as a means of conveying another 'low philological jest': when Sam Gamgee and Ted Sandyman discuss the plausibility of Sam's cousin Hal's report of tree-like giants in the North-farthing, they both thus unwittingly name these giants Ents (1a). Treebeard, the only non-hobbit to use the form *ain't*, is made to indulge in a quibble of Shakespearean proportions (1b).

(1) a. 'But what about these Tree-men, these giants, as you might call them?' [...] 'Your Hal's always saying that he's seen things; and maybe he sees things that **ain't** there.' [...] 'What he saw *was* an elm tree, as like as not.' 'But this one was *walking*, I tell you; and there **ain't** no elm tree on the North Moors. (Ted and Sam, LotR 1 II:17,20,22,23)

---

5   The word *lass* is actually not recorded from the Survey informants in Warwickshire/Oxfordshire (who all use *wench* or *girl*), only from the more northerly West Midland counties of Derbyshire, Shropshire, and Staffordshire.

b. There are Ents and Ents, you know; or there are things that look like Ents but **ain't**, as you might say. (Treebeard, LotR 3 IV:40)

Table 1 lists a number of the more frequent non-standard English forms used in hobbit dialogue and the corresponding forms recorded from the Survey informants in Warwickshire and Oxfordshire. The table is merely intended to give an indication of the range of attested Warwickshire/Oxfordshire forms that are used to represent Shiretalk. It makes no pretence to completeness, the more so since it is impossible to draw a hard and fast line between regionally and stylistically (colloquial, slang, vulgar, etc.) marked variants. For example, *noodle* and *numbskull* (both meaning 'fool', 'simpleton') appear in the *Basic Material* from the Northern West Midlands (*BM* 586), yet both words are listed in the *Oxford English Dictionary* (s.v. **noodle** and **numskull**) without being labelled dialectal.

There is, however, one construction used to characterize Shiretalk which is not represented in the Dialect Survey data from the Warwickshire/Oxfordshire area, indeed not from the West Midland region. This is the contracted auxiliary construction *'ll not* (as in *I'll not deny*), contrasting with *won't* and *will not*. *LAE* shows it confined to a small area in the North of England (Northumberland, northern Durham and northern Cumberland) with stray occurrences in Lancashire (*LAE* map 49). Trudgill (1978:13) claims that "the further north one goes [...] the more likely one is to find the alternative construction type" (i.e. *'ll not*). Even so, the construction does occur in the West Midlands as well, although it may not have been sufficiently frequent there to have presented itself as the first alternative for the Survey informants from the West Midlands.

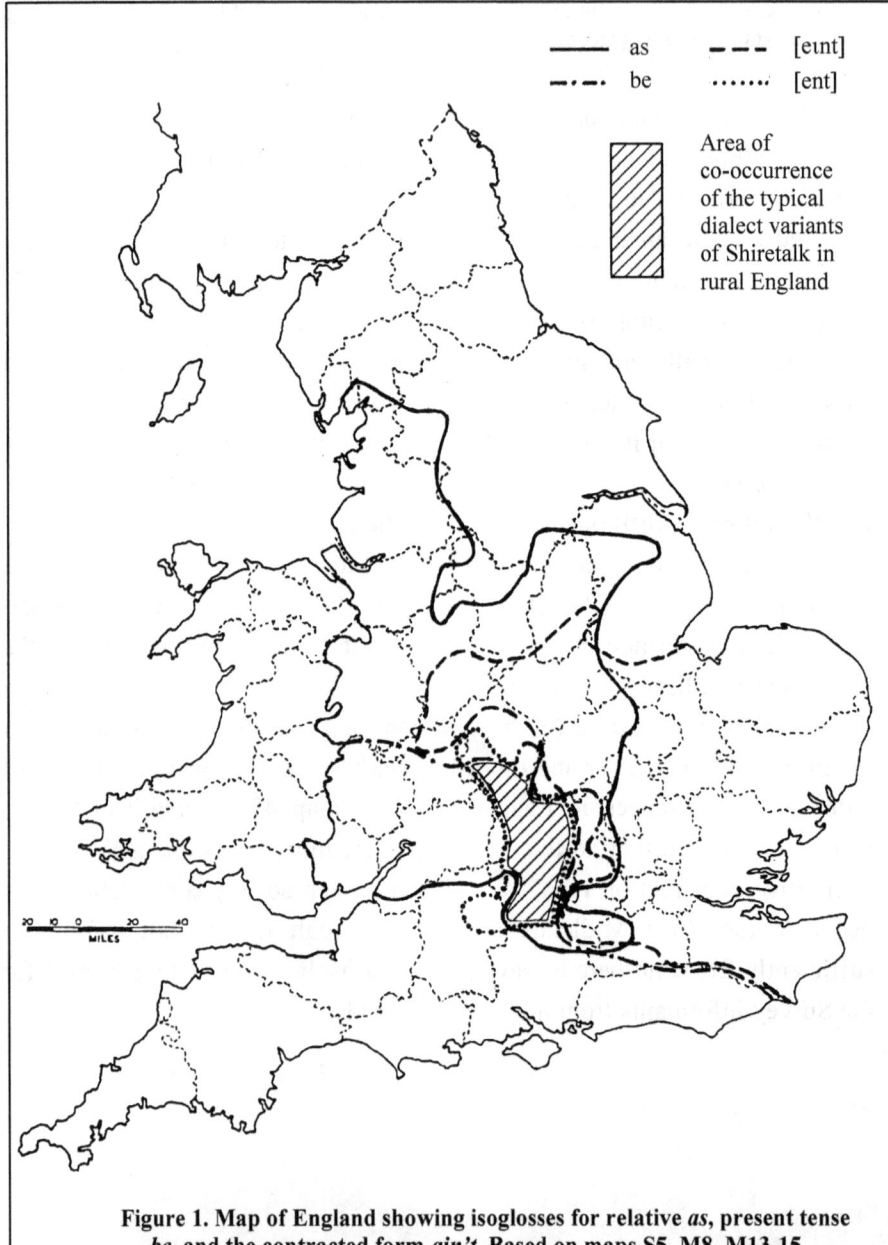

Figure 1. Map of England showing isoglosses for relative *as*, present tense *be*, and the contracted form *ain't*. Based on maps S5, M8, M13-15, and M19 in *The Linguistic Atlas of England*.

LotR forms	Typical Survey forms from Warwickshire/Oxfordshire
agin 'near', 'beside'	əgɪn
a-going	əgɷˑɪn
ain't	ɛnt, ɛnˀ
a-purpose	ə pəːpəs, ə pəːᵗpəs
as *rel. pron.* 'who(m)', 'which'	əz
(they/you) **be** '(they/you) are'	ðɛɪ, juː biː
(he/it) **don't**	doɷnt, doːnt
drownd '(to) drown'	drɛɷnd, dɾaɷnd
(I) **dunno** '(I) don't know'	a dɷ no, ʌʏ dʌ noɷ, ɔɪ dɷ noɷ
durstn't 'did not dare'	dəsnt, dʌsnt, dəᵗʈṣn̪t̪
'ee 'you' (subj.)	wɔᵗːn̪t̪ iː 'weren't 'ee', duː iː 'do 'ee'
'you' (obj.)	pliːzd tə siː ɪ 'pleased to see 'ee'
'em 'them'	əm, ɷm
et 'eaten'	ɛt
etten 'eaten'	ɛtn, ɛˀn
hisself 'himself'	ɪzsɛɬf
lay 'lie'	lɛɪ, leː
learn 'teach'	ləᵗːn̪, laᵗːn̪
naught, nought, nowt 'nothing'	nɔɷt, noɷt
o' 'of'	pæɷnd ə tɛɪ 'pound of tea'
	plɛnˀɪ ə mʌnɪ 'plenty of money'
didn't ought to be/have	dɪdn ɔːt ə v
taters 'potatoes'	tɛɪtəz, teːtəᵗz
they has/goes	ðɛɪ az, ðə goɷz
'tis, 'twas	tɪz, twəz
took 'taken'	tɷk
weskit 'waistcoat'	wɛskɪt, wɛskət
yonder 'there'	jɔndə, jɒndəᵗ

Table 1. Some non-standard English forms used in dialogue by Shire hobbits and Breelanders in LotR, and their corresponding forms in the dialect of Warwickshire/Oxfordshire as given in *The Survey of English Dialects: Basic Material*, vol. 2.

2 SOCIAL CLASS MARKERS

2.1 Negation

In English sentences containing an indefinite noun phrase in predicative position the sentence negation can take three different forms, as shown in example (2): analytic negation, synthetic negation, and double negation.

(2) a. *not any~*:   I didn't see anything.   [analytic negation]
    b. *no~*:   I saw nothing.   [synthetic negation]
    c. *not no~*:   I didn't see nothing.   [double negation]

Double negation, ever since it came under attack from normative eighteenth century grammarians as being 'illogical', has been relegated to non-standard status; early twentieth century grammarians describe it as typical of "popular speech" (Curme and Kurath 1931:139) or "vulgar speakers" (Jespersen 1940:452), whereas more recent works use less value-laden terms like "nonstandard English" (Quirk et al. 1985:787). Partridge (1947:200) states that an example such as *I don't know nothing* "is psychologically defensible but contrary to the present idiom of the educated".[6]

There is a marked difference between hobbits and non-hobbits in the use of different negation types: non-hobbits strongly favour synthetic negation, whereas hobbits tend to use double and analytic negation, as is shown in Table 2.[7]

---

[6] Partridge, whose *Usage and Abusage. A Guide to Good English* first appeared in 1947, will be referred to from time to time below as a good example of a prescriptive grammarian of Tolkien's generation.

[7] Excluded from the data in Table 2 is one example in which Bilbo quotes Gandalf (using synthetic negation), since it is difficult to know whether the actual wording is Bilbo's or Gandalf's. On the other hand, four examples in which quoted speaker and quoter belong to the same speaker category have been included (Butterbur quoting Gandalf (2 exx.), Frodo quoting Bilbo (1 ex.), and Gandalf quoting Saruman (1 ex.)). In the same way, quotes across speaker category (or subcategory) boundaries (Bilbo/Gandalf, Butterbur/Gandalf) have been excluded from Table 3, and all the quoted examples have been excluded from Tables 4-6.

	Double	Analytic	Synthetic	Σ
Hobbits	41 (15.4%)	75 (28.2%)	150 (56.4%)	266
Non-hobbits	7 (1.6%)	40 (8.9%)	401 (89.5%)	449

Table 2. The use of different types of negation in LotR.[8]

A closer look at different subgroups (Table 3) reveals that the different negation types function as clear class markers among hobbits: only WC hobbits use double negation, whereas LC hobbits use analytic negation to a greater extent than any other subgroup among hobbits or non-hobbits.

	Double	Analytic	Synthetic	Σ
HOBBITS				
LC		59 (36.6%)	102 (63.4%)	161
WC	41 (39.1%)	16 (15.2%)	48 (45.7%)	105
NON-HOBBITS				
Breelanders	5 (45.5%)		6 (54.5%)	11
Gollum	1 (14.3%)	1 (14.3%)	5 (71.4%)	7
Orcs	1 (4.0%)	6 (24.0%)	18 (72.0%)	25
Ents		2 (15.4%)	11 (84.6%)	13
Wizards		16 (12.4%)	113 (87.6%)	129
Gondoreans		6 (12.0%)	44 (88.0%)	50
Rangers		4 (6.5%)	58 (93.5%)	62
Elves		2 (5.4%)	35 (94.6%)	37
Dwarves		2 (5.0%)	38 (95.0%)	40
Rohirrim			59	59

Table 3. The use of different types of negation by different groups of speakers in LotR.

---

8 Great care has been taken to ensure that the quantitative data presented in this paper are correct. It must be remembered, however, that the relevant examples have been identified by means of text reading, and it is consequently not impossible that a few examples may have escaped my notice. This is the kind of uncertainty that we have to put up with until the Tolkien œuvre is available in machine-readable form for research purposes. The discussion of quantitative data in the present paper is based on the assumption that the data are correct.

In the non-hobbit category the Breelanders (chiefly represented by Barliman Butterbur) are singled out by their high frequency of double negation, placing them on roughly the same level as Shire WC hobbits. Otherwise double negation is used by Gollum and by an orc (Shagrat), but only to a negligible extent. All non-hobbit groups (except Breelanders) are characterized by their very high frequencies (over 70%) of synthetic negation.

If we go one step further and consider the use of negation in the speech of individual characters (Table 4), a picture emerges of both consistency and variation. The individual non-hobbit characters (Butterbur excluded) exhibit the greatest consistency: they all rely primarily on synthetic negation, in a few cases (Théoden, Éomer, Éowyn, Saruman, Denethor) exclusively. Among hobbits, well-documented LC speakers consistently use analytic negation more frequently than non-hobbits. WC hobbits, finally, exhibit the greatest variation, but five out of eight speakers use double negation to a great extent. Thus, Butterbur's use of negation is closer to that of WC hobbits than to non-hobbits.

	Double	Analytic	Synthetic	Σ
LC				
Lobelia			1	1
Pippin		10 (23.8%)	32 (76.2%)	42
Frodo		30 (38.0%)	49 (62.0%)	79
Merry		13 (43.3%)	17 (56.7%)	30
Bilbo		4 (66.7%)	2 (33.3%)	6
Fatty		1		1
WC				
Hob Hayward	2			2
Gatekeeper	1			1
Gaffer Gamgee	5 (71.4%)		2 (28.6%)	7
Farmer Cotton	7 (50.0%)	1 (7.1%)	6 (42.9%)	14
Sam Gamgee	26 (36.1%)	11 (15.3%)	35 (48.6%)	72
Farmer Maggot		2 (40.0%)	3 (60.0%)	5
Ted Sandyman		2 (66.7%)	1 (33.3%)	3
Tom Cotton, Jr.			1	1

Table 4. The use of different types of negation by selected characters in LotR.

	Double	Analytic	Synthetic	Σ
NON-HOBBITS				
Butterbur	5 (50.0%)		5 (50.0%)	10
Treebeard		2 (15.4%)	11 (84.6%)	13
Gandalf		16 (13.6%)	102 (86.4%)	118
Faramir		3 (12.5%)	21 (87.5%)	24
Legolas		1 (6.7%)	14 (93.3%)	15
Aragorn		4 (6.5%)	58 (93.5%)	62
Gimli		2 (5.1%)	37 (94.9%)	39
Théoden			23	23
Éomer			16	16
Éowyn			10	10
Saruman			10	10
Denethor			5	5

Table 4. The use of different types of negation by selected characters in LotR (cont.).

In the primary world it is a well-known fact that speakers of different (but to some extent similar) varieties of a language tend to modify their speech in the direction of the variety/varieties of their interlocutors. The same kind of linguistic accommodation[9] can be discerned among LotR speakers. Both Gandalf and Aragorn, for example, tend to modify their use of sentence negation in the direction of the speech of LC hobbits when speaking to hobbits: all of Aragorn's examples of analytic negation occur in his conversation with Frodo and his party at the *Prancing Pony* in Bree, and Gandalf's frequency of analytic negation is at its highest during his conversation with Frodo in LotR 1 II (Gandalf/1 in Table 5). It is considerably lower after his reappearance in Rivendell up to his fall in Moria (Gandalf/2), and lower still after his second reappearance in Fangorn (Gandalf/3).

This change in Aragorn's and Gandalf's use of negation could, alternatively, be interpreted as an indication of Tolkien's increasing preference for synthetic negation as his work on LotR proceeded. But such an

---

[9] For an introduction to accommodation theory, see Giles and Smith 1979.

interpretation is made untenable by the fact that other characters exhibit different patterns of change. Frodo's use of sentence negation is at its most typical for an LC hobbit in the early and late parts of LotR (before the breaking of the Fellowship, Frodo/1, and after the destruction of the Ring, Frodo/5 in Table 5); it is modified in the direction of non-hobbit speakers in the intermediate episodes (Frodo/2-4). While he is together with Faramir in Ithilien his use of synthetic negation goes up to a hundred per cent (Frodo/3).

Sam, finally, shows a tendency to accommodate to Frodo's LC usage when they are journeying together in the wilderness: he never uses analytic negation before the breaking of the Fellowship (Sam/1 in Table 5), but in over twenty per cent of the cases from Emyn Muil to Mount Doom (Sam/2). It is noteworthy that this move in the direction of Frodo's 'normal' usage is taking place at the same time as Frodo is moving **away** from it, yielding almost identical figures for analytic negation for Sam and Frodo. However, since Sam never gives up using double negation, the typical feature of WC hobbit speech, and since Frodo increases his use of synthetic negation beyond Sam's level, their language varieties nevertheless remain distinct while all this accommodation is going on.

	Double	Analytic	Synthetic	Σ
Gandalf/1		11 (39.3%)	17 (60.7%)	28
Gandalf/2		3 (7.7%)	36 (92.3%)	39
Gandalf/3		2 (3.9%)	49 (96.1%)	51
Frodo/1		17 (63.0%)	10 (37.0%)	27
Frodo/2		3 (21.4%)	11 (78.6%)	14
Frodo/3			10	10
Frodo/4		5 (29.4%)	12 (70.6%)	17
Frodo/5		5 (50.0%)	5 (50.0%)	10
Sam/1	11 (57.9%)		8 (42.1%)	19
Sam/2	4 (27.4%)	11 (21.6%)	26 (51.0%)	51
Sam/3	1 (50.0%)		1 (50.0%)	2

Table 5. Variable use of sentence negation by three characters in LotR.

Barliman Butterbur is a character whose use of sentence negation merits some discussion. Although he is a man, his use of negation agrees well with the WC hobbit pattern (Table 4). This is actually true of his use of other variables as well. The reason why he speaks like a WC hobbit is presumably to be found in the social structure of the Bree region, where men and hobbits lived together "on friendly terms, minding their own affairs in their own ways, but both rightly regarding themselves as necessary parts of the Bree-folk. Nowhere else in the world was this peculiar (but excellent) arrangement to be found." (LotR 1 IX:4)

Two hypotheses can be set up to account for Butterbur's speech habits: either men and hobbits in Bree spoke in (more or less) the same way, or else Butterbur, who naturally was acquainted with hobbit speech in Bree (which at least syntactically was close to Shire WC speech), sought to ingratiate himself with his hobbit visitors by accommodating to their speech. Tolkien's own comments are not very helpful: when vocabulary differences between Bree and the Shire are mentioned,[10] it is never clear whether the Bree dialect is that of the hobbits, the men, or both.

The second hypothesis can, unfortunately, never be tested, since all the relevant samples of Butterbur's speech come from conversations with hobbits; we do not know how he would speak to non-hobbits. A point in favour of the first hypothesis, on the other hand, is the fact that Frodo seemed to regard all Breelanders as talking alike, since he did not qualify his comment on Strider's speech one way or the other: "You began to talk to me like the Bree-folk [...]" (LotR 1 X:31). In the following, I will assume, without further comment, that men and hobbits in Bree formed a single speech community, and that Butterbur is a typical representative of that speech community.

To sum up, all the three negation variants function as group-identifying indices: double negation by its mere presence in WC hobbit speech, analytic and synthetic negation by their dominance in LC hobbit speech and in non-hobbit speech, respectively. This basic pattern can be blurred, however, as

---

10 LotR 1 IX:46, App. D 16§, App. F II:9, 13.

some characters modify their speech in order to accommodate to the speech of their interlocutors.

2.2 Agreement

In principle, the rule for subject-verb agreement in English is simple and straightforward: in the present tense, a suffix *-s* (sometimes *-es*) is added to the stem of a main verb if it has a third person singular subject, otherwise the verb stem is used without a suffix. With the verb BE, a somewhat richer paradigm is available, but again an *s*-form (*is* in the present tense, *was* in the past) is used in contrast with *s*-less forms (present tense *am/are*, past tense *were*).

In many (non-standard) regional and social dialects of English, however, this agreement rule does not apply: *s*-forms may be used with subjects which are not in the third person singular, and third person singular subjects may be used with *s*-less forms. Even in standard English, however, there is one context in which *s*-forms can be used with non-third person subjects, namely in existential *there*-constructions in informal style (*There's hundreds of people there* or *There are hundreds of people there*; cf. Quirk et al. 1985:756). Such constructions are occasionally used by Tolkien in the narrative text in LotR (*There was nearly two hundred of them*, LotR 6 VIII:155); when they occur in dialogue (23 times altogether), they have been classified as examples of standard agreement.[11]

In the speech of WC hobbits in the Shire, as well as in the Bree dialect, several instances of non-standard present or past tense subject-verb agreement (e.g. *he don't, I knows, you was*) can be found, as shown in (3) (emphasis added). This type of non-standard agreement is used only by WC

---

11 Not even Partridge (1947:334) – in other cases very quick to condemn non-standard forms as 'illiterate' – seems particularly disturbed by this construction: "**there**, introductory, is apt to cause the verb to fail to agree with the subject in number, [...] It is difficult to avoid the impression that these, and other, authors subconsciously regard *there* as a noun (therefore singular), hence as the subject of the sentence."

hobbits and Breelanders, never by LC hobbits. It also occurs once in the speech of Tom Bombadil (*if he don't behave himself*, LotR 1 VI:80).

(3) a. [...] **he don't** tell nobody what cause he has to hurry. (Butterbur, LotR 1 IX:52)
   b. [...], not if **I knows** Bill Ferny. (Bob, LotR 1 XI:29)
   c. What if **you comes** to a place [...]? (Sam, LotR 4 I:36)
   d. **They moves** about and **comes** and **goes**. (Farmer Cotton, LotR 6 VIII:135)

A slightly different type of non-standard agreement involves the use of the form *be* as a present tense form with plural subjects, corresponding to standard English *are*. It is used once by each of Gaffer Gamgee and his crony Daddy Twofoot (4 a, b); the only other example from hobbit speech occurs when Tom Cotton Jr. tells the anecdote about Lobelia's encounter with the ruffians (4c).

(4) a. That's a dark bad place, if **half the tales be** true. (Daddy Twofoot, LotR 1 I:11)
   b. [...] in foreign parts, where **there be mountains** of gold [...] (Gaffer Gamgee, LotR 1 I:20)
   c. "Where **be you** a-going?" says she. (Tom Cotton Jr. quoting Lobelia Sackville-Baggins, LotR 6 VIII:175)
   d. [...] it must have been near dark when **this fellow come** up the Hill and found him taking the air [...] (Sam, LotR 1 III:93)

Apart from present tense *be* the only *s*-less form used by LotR characters in non-standard subject-verb agreement is *he/it don't*; other verbs always turn up as *s*-forms in such a context. An apparent exception is shown in (4d), where *come* is not a (historical) present tense form but actually a past tense form. This is the typical past tense form (pronounced /kɷm/) in the Survey of English Dialects material from the West Midlands (Orton and Barry 1971:994; Orton et al. 1978, map M51). It is the only example of its kind found in LotR.

Table 6 shows the use of standard and non-standard variants by WC hobbits, Breelanders and Tom Bombadil. Non-standard agreement is never used by LC hobbits, nor is it used by any non-hobbits except Butterbur and Tom Bombadil.

	Standard agreement	**Non-standard agreement**	**Finite *be***	**Σ**
Tom Cotton Jr.	15 (83.3%)	3 (16.7%)		18
Hob Hayward	19 (90.5%)	2 (9.5%)		21
Ted Sandyman	29 (93.5%)	2 (6.5%)		31
Robin Smallburrow	31 (93.9%)	2 (6.1%)		33
Farmer Cotton	114 (94.2%)	7 (5.8%)		121
Gaffer Gamgee	82 (95.3%)	3 (3.5%)	1 (1.2%)	86
Farmer Maggot	75 (97.4%)	2 (2.6%)		77
Sam Gamgee	1318 (98.7%)	18 (1.3%)		1336
Daddy Twofoot	3 (75.0%)		1 (25.0%)	4
Shirriff	16			16
Sam/Gaffer Gamgee(a)	13			13
Rose Cotton	11			11
Old Noakes	8			8
Tookland messenger	6			6
WC hobbits (unid.)	6			6
Sandyman Sr.	4			4
Stranger	4			4
Mrs. Cotton	2			2
Old gaffer at inn	2			2
Gatekeeper	1			1
Old gaffer, Frogmorton	1			1
Σ WC hobbits	1760 (97.72%)	39 (2.17%)	2 (0.11%)	1801
Bob	2 (66.7%)	1 (33.3%)		3
Nob	6 (85.7%)	1 (14.3%)		7
Butterbur	270 (99.3%)	2 (0.7%)		272
Harry Goatleaf	9			9
Bill Ferny	7			7
Mugwort	5			5
Bree hobbits (unid.)	2			2
Gatekeeper, Bree	1			1
Σ Breelanders	302 (98.7%)	4 (1.3%)		306
Tom Bombadil	98 (95.1%)	1 (1.0%)	4 (3.9%)	103

(a) This notation is used to refer to a case where the first character quotes the second character.

Table 6. Users and number of occurrences of standard and non-standard subject-verb agreement in LotR.

That the use of non-standard agreement in constructions with main verbs functions as a group-identifying index, identifying the speaker as belonging to the working class, seems obvious. The use of finite *be*, on the other hand, does not seem to have the same function. The fact that this form is never used by Sam Gamgee – otherwise the user *par préférence* of WC forms – makes it doubtful that it is meant to identify the speaker as a member of the working class. Instead it may be noted that it is only used by old speakers – Gaffer Gamgee (93-94 years), Daddy Twofoot (presumably the same age), and Lobelia Sackville-Baggins (100-101 years), which suggests that it represents an antiquated form of speech in the Shire.[12] It is never used by Bilbo (128-129 years), presumably because it had been confined to members of the working class in his youth. How, in that case, can we explain Lobelia's use of *be*, since she must be regarded as a member of the leisure class?

If we choose to regard (4c) as an inaccurate quotation, with the actual wording supplied by Tom Cotton Jr., we have to give up the interpretation of finite *be* as an antiquated feature. It seems more attractive to me to assume that this *be* is Lobelia's own word, and that it is her heated exchange with the ruffians that makes her forget herself to such an extent that vulgarisms current in her youth creep into her speech (cf. also her use of *a-going*, section 2.4.1 below). The use of 'coarse' language in unguarded moments would certainly be consistent with her general image of old harridan (compare, for example, the way she rides roughshod over Frodo the day after the Great Party, LotR 1 I:147-155).

2.3 Contraction

2.3.1 *ain't*

A non-standard contracted verb form that is widespread in the English-speaking world is *ain't*, which can represent a negated present tense form of either BE or HAVE. Words fail Partridge (1947:19) in his condemnation of

---

12 It may be pointed out that finite *be* is used by only one non-hobbit, namely Tom Bombadil (four times). He is certainly old enough to use a form characteristic of an older hobbit generation.

this form: "**ain't** for *isn't* (colloquial) or *is not* (Standard English) is an error so illiterate that I blush to record it. As for *ain't* for *hasn't* (*has not*) or *haven't* (*have not*) ...!" (original ellipsis).

To the extent that the form *ain't* occurs in LotR, it is used only as a negated present tense form of BE (never of HAVE). In the data presented in Table 7 below, the use of *ain't* is contrasted with all other forms of negated present tense BE (e.g. *is not*, *isn't*, *'s not*, all of which are used by Butterbur); no functional difference between the other types of negation of BE can be discerned, and they are therefore treated as one category (–AIN'T).

In the Shire, *ain't* is used only by WC hobbits: Sam Gamgee, Gaffer Gamgee, and Ted Sandyman, as illustrated in (5) (cf. also (1a) above).

(5) a. That **ain't** no secret. (Gaffer Gamgee, LotR 1 III:37)
    b. But nothing's wrong. Though it **ain't** quite what I'd call right. (Sam, LotR 4 IV:50)

This form is never used by LC hobbits or non-hobbits, with the exception of Treebeard, who uses it once in a conversation with Merry and Pippin (example (1b)). His expression *as you might say* may give the impression that he is deliberately using a typical hobbit expression. However, when Treebeard utters (1b) he has only just learnt about the existence of hobbits, and could consequently have no previous knowledge of hobbit speech characteristics. As a matter of fact, *(as) you might say* occurs five times in Treebeard's conversation with Merry and Pippin in LotR 3 IV; this may well be meant to suggest that Treebeard, although he apparently has a far-reaching command of 'outside languages', is nevertheless speaking a foreign language (the Common Speech) in which some phrases may not come altogether naturally to him. Both he and Quickbeam are represented as using an informal style of the Common Speech, which is presumably the reason for his use of *ain't*. (For an alternative, or perhaps complementary, explanation, see section 1.3 above.)

	+AIN'T	−AIN'T
Ted Sandyman	1 (50.0%)	1 (50.0%)
Gaffer Gamgee	1 (33.3%)	2 (66.7%)
Sam Gamgee	7 (14.0%)	43 (86.0%)
Farmer Cotton		3
Farmer Maggot		3
Hob Hayward		2
Robin Smallburrow		2
WC hobbits (unid.)		2
Σ WC hobbits	9 (13.4%)	58 (86.6%)
Butterbur		9
Treebeard	1 (50.0%)	1 (50.0%)

Table 7. The use of *ain't* (+AIN'T) versus other negated present tense forms of BE (−AIN'T) by WC hobbits, Butterbur and Treebeard.

2.3.2 *'ll not*

The construction *will not* can be contracted in two different ways: either as *won't* (negator contraction) or *'ll not* (auxiliary contraction). The distribution of the three variants in LotR is shown in table 8 below. A very clear distribution pattern emerges: the form *'ll not* is used (in variation with *won't*) in the speech of WC hobbits and Butterbur, and, on one occasion, by the orc Shagrat. The majority of individual speakers use *won't* exclusively: hobbits, Breelanders, ruffians, orcs. Variation between *won't* and *will not* is exhibited by three LC hobbits and Gandalf. Exclusive use of *will not*, finally, is confined to a few high-mimetic characters: elves, Gondoreans, Rohirrim. There can be no doubt of the indexical function of the variants. A few typical examples of the use of *'ll not* are shown in (6).

(6) a. And then **he'll not** leave you again. (Sam, LotR 3 X:40)
　b. **You'll not** have need to go near the old Hobbiton village over Water. (Farmer Cotton, LotR 6 VIII:166)
　c. **I'll not** light my lanterns till I turn for home. (Farmer Maggot, LotR 1 IV:108)
　d. **I'll not** deny we should be glad to have you about for a bit. (Butterbur, LotR 6 VII:35)

	'll not	*won't*	*will not*
Butterbur	4 (44.4%)	5 (55.6%)	
Bob		1	
Gatekeeper, Bree		1	
Σ Bree	4 (36.4%)	7 (63.6%)	
Farmer Maggot	2 (33.3%)	4 (66.7%)	
Gatekeeper		1	
Σ Eastfarthing	2 (28.6%)	5 (71.4%)	
Farmer Cotton	1 (33.3%)	2 (66.7%)	
Sam Gamgee	1 (4.5%)	21 (95.5%)	
Gaffer Gamgee		1	
Sam/Gaffer		1	
Ted Sandyman		1	
Σ Central Shire	2 (7.1%)	26 (92.9%)	
Shagrat	1 (20.0%)	4 (80.0%)	
Merry		7	
Bilbo		4	
Snaga		3	
Tom Bombadil		2	
Gorbag		2	
Uglúk		2	
Butterbur/Gandalf		1	
Grishnákh		1	
Ruffian		1	
Small orc		1	
Frodo		13 (76.5%)	4 (23.5%)
Pippin		5 (62.5%)	3 (37.5%)
Fatty Bolger		1 (50.0%)	1 (50.0%)
Gandalf		2 (28.6%)	5 (71.4%)
Denethor			4
Ingold			2
Gondoreans (unid.)			2
Elrond			1
Galadriel			1
Pippin/Treebeard			1
Rider of Rohan			1
Saruman			1

Table 8. The use of the variants *'ll not*, *won't* and *will not* in LotR.

The data from the Shire and Bree suggest that *'ll not* functions not only as a marker of WC speech but also as a regional group-identifying index among speakers in these regions. Its frequency of occurrence in the speech of documented speaker groups increases from west to east: as suggested by the group averages in Table 8, it is lowest in the speech of characters from the central Shire (Farmer Cotton, Sam, Gaffer Gamgee, Ted Sandyman), higher in the Eastfarthing (Farmer Maggot, the gatekeeper at the Brandywine Bridge), and highest in the speech of Breelanders (Butterbur, Bob, the nameless gatekeeper in LotR 6). We can thus envisage a dialect continuum stretching across the Shire and incorporating Bree. There is plenty of evidence to support such an interpretation of the data:

i) The outlook of WC hobbits was extremely parochial, as shown by the following quotations: "It beats me why any Baggins of Hobbiton should go looking for a wife away there in Buckland, where folks are so queer." (Old Noakes of Bywater, LotR 1 I:10); "Not that the Brandybucks of Buckland live *in* the Old Forest; but they're a queer breed, seemingly." (Gaffer Gamgee, LotR 1 I:12); "[Sam] had a natural distrust of the inhabitants of other parts of the Shire" (LotR 1 IV:81); "You should never have gone mixing yourself up with Hobbiton folk, Mr. Frodo. Folk are queer up there." (Farmer Maggot, LotR 1 IV:94); "The Shire-hobbits referred to those of Bree [...] as Outsiders, and took very little interest in them, considering them dull and uncouth." (LotR 1 IX:5). Such attitudes are consistent with a situation in which WC hobbits formed dense local networks (cf. Milroy 1980:21) and there was little contact between speakers from different localities. As a consequence of the relative isolation of each local network we can expect to find considerable differences between local dialects within the area.

ii) As mentioned in 2.1 above, we know that dialect differences existed with respect to lexical items. It seems reasonable to assume, then, that syntactic differences existed as well.

iii) In British English the variant *'ll not* actually functions as a regional group-identifying index: it is most commonly used in Northern England and Scotland (Trudgill 1978:13; cf. also Orton and Halliday 1963:1018-19, where *'ll not* is recorded in Northumberland, Cumberland, Durham and Lancashire). Furthermore, in popular fiction it is used as a stereotype to indicate the regional origin of speakers (it is typically put in the mouth of

Scotsmen; see, for example, Christie 1980:38, 43, 100 (Colin McNabb); 174 (Detective-Constable McCrae)). For this reason it should be easily recognizable in its indexical function when used by speakers in LotR as well. Against this it might be argued that Frodo and Merry never use *'ll not*, although they both grew up in Buckland. But this is most likely due to the fact that they are both LC hobbits. Assuming that the linguistic situation in the Shire resembles that in England in this respect (which seems highly likely), we would expect regional variation to occur only in WC speech (cf. Trudgill 1974:40-41).

2.4 Verb constructions

Three different verb constructions have an indexical function in the speech of LotR hobbits: prefixed present and past participles, and verb phrases with *ought to*.

2.4.1 Present participle

In many parts of the English-speaking world a non-standard variant of the present participle with the prefix *a-* (as in *a-coming, a-going*) is used in variation with the standard form of the present participle (*coming, going*) (Trudgill 1978:15). According to Partridge (1947:9), "[i]t occurs [...] in illiterate speech such as Cockney 'I arst you wot you was a-doin' of' (D. Sayers), and American Southern Mountain 'He's a-singin' a love song' (ballad)". Historically, the *a-* represents a reduced form of the preposition *on*, used with a verbal noun ending in *-ing* as a forerunner of the modern progressive construction.

In LotR this verb form is primarily used by Tom Bombadil (cf. table 9), but it is also used by two WC hobbits (Sam and Farmer Cotton), as shown in (7). The prefixed participle is also used once by Tom Cotton Jr., quoting Lobelia Sackville-Baggins (4c). It was claimed in section 2.2 above that it makes best sense to regard this as an accurate quotation of Lobelia's utterance. This example notwithstanding, the variant is obviously a marker

The Speech of the Individual and of the Community in LotR   37

of WC hobbit speech, since it is never used by any other LC hobbit. (In table 9 the quote from Lobelia is not included in the total figure for LC hobbits.)

(7) a. Look here, Cock-Robin! You're Hobbiton-bred and ought to have more sense, coming **a-waylaying** Mr. Frodo and all. (Sam, LotR 6 VIII:51)
 b. They're always **a-hammering** and **a-letting** out a smoke and a stench, [...] (Farmer Cotton, LotR 6 VIII:173)

	V*ing*	*a*-V*ing*
Tom Bombadil	13 (72.2%)	5 (27.8%)
Tom Cotton/Lobelia		1
Farmer Cotton	21 (91.3%)	2 (8.7%)
Sam Gamgee	184 (98.4%)	3 (1.6%)
Farmer Maggot	24	
Gaffer Gamgee	10	
Robin Smallburrow	9	
Shirriff	8	
Hob Hayward	5	
Rose Cotton	2	
Ted Sandyman	2	
Tookland messenger	2	
Maggot/Ringwraith	1	
Mrs. Cotton	1	
Mrs. Maggot	1	
Old Noakes	1	
Tom Cotton, Jr.	1	
WC hobbits (unid.)	1	
Σ WC hobbits	273 (91.3%)	7 (2.5%)
Butterbur	39	
Harry Goatleaf	2	
Nob	2	
Σ Breelanders	43	
Bilbo	9	
Merry	3	
Pippin	3	
Frodo	2	
Otho	1	
Σ LC hobbits	18	

Table 9. The use of standard (V*ing*) and prefixed (*a*-V*ing*) present participle forms by characters in LotR.

2.4.2 Past participle

Like the present participle, the past participle can be variably preceded by a particle *a* (written *a'* in LotR, either as a separate word or combined with the following participle), as illustrated in (8). Partridge (1947:9) describes the prefixed form, not unexpectedly, as "illiterate". This particle can have two different origins: it can be a reduced form of the auxiliary HAVE, as in (8a), or it can be formally superfluous, as in (8b). Since there are so few examples in LotR, it seems pointless to treat these two types separately. Unlike the prefixed present participle, this non-standard participle form is used exclusively by WC hobbits. (Table 10 gives the relevant data for this speaker category alone; past participles as such are, needless to say, common enough among all types of speakers.) It is not even very widespread among this speaker category; possible interpretations of this limited distribution will be discussed in section 3 below.

(8) a. I should **a' passed** you in the street [...] (Farmer Cotton, LotR 6 VIII:116)
 b. I didn't know as anything grew in Mordor! But if I had **a'known**, this is just what I'd have looked for. [...] Wish I'd **a'put** that mail-shirt on. (Sam, LotR 6 II:10)

	V*ed*	*a'*V*ed*
Gaffer Gamgee	11 (91.67%)	1 (8.33%)
Sam Gamgee	40 (93.02%)	3 (6.98%)
Farmer Cotton	19 (95.00%)	1 (5.00%)
Farmer Maggot	7	
Robin Smallburrow	5	
Ted Sandyman	4	
Rose Cotton	3	
Tookland messenger	3	
WC hobbits (unidentified)	2	
Hob Hayward	1	
Old gaffer, Frogmorton	1	
Old Noakes	1	
Sam/Rose	1	
Shirriff	1	
Stranger from Michel Delving	1	
Tom Cotton Jr.	1	

Table 10. The use of standard (V*ed*) and prefixed (*a'*V*ed*) present participle forms by WC hobbits in LotR.

2.4.3 *ought to*

Originating historically as a main verb, *ought (to)* can only be treated as an auxiliary in modern standard English. Thus, the negative and interrogative counterparts of *he ought to go* are *he ought not to go* and *ought he to go?*, respectively. Many native speakers find these constructions unwieldy and tend to avoid *ought to* altogether, relying instead on the more or less synonymous auxiliary *should*. In non-standard varieties of English, however, a different strategy is adopted: *ought* is treated as a main verb, and will thus occur with *do*-periphrasis in negative and interrogative contexts (*he didn't ought to go, did he ought to go?*). In the Shire, such constructions are found only in Sam's (four times) and Gaffer Gamgee's speech (once), as illustrated in (9). Example (9b), incidentally, contains a heavy dose of markers of WC speech: apart from non-standard *ought to* we also find double negative and prefixed past participle.

(9) a. I **didn't ought to** have left my blanket behind. (Sam, LotR 6 III:50)
　b. You **didn't never ought to** have a' sold Bag End, [....] (Gaffer Gamgee, LotR 6 VIII:183)

2.5 Relative pronouns

The use of relative pronouns in English offers wide scope for variation. In standard English, three different pronoun types are available: *wh*-pronouns (*who/whom/which*), the indeclinable *that* and, finally, Ø (zero, i.e. absence of pronoun to mark the status of the following clause). In various non-standard varieties two other relative pronouns can also be found, namely *as* and *what*.

　The selection of pronoun type in the individual clause is, however, determined not only by the variety of English (standard versus non-standard), but also by the different types of clause in which the pronoun may be used. Again, three major types can be recognized: restrictive relative clause (10a), non-restrictive relative clause (10b), and what we may call a cleft relative (the subordinate clause in a cleft sentence construction, as in

(10c)). The difference between the three types is related to the information expressed: the restrictive relative clause expresses information that should enable the hearer/reader to identify the referent of the antecedent (*which arm?*), whereas the non-restrictive clause merely supplies additional information about an already identified referent. A cleft sentence, finally, is used to single out one clause element and present it as new information (or merely emphasize its high information value: *the shield arm* in (10c)); the cleft relative presents information that is assumed to be known.

(10) a. The arm **that was broken** has been tended with due skill (Aragorn, LotR 5 VIII:81)
  b. [...] how tall and fair was Eorl the Young, **who rode down out of the North** (Aragorn, LotR 3 VI:17)
  c. It is the shield-arm **that is maimed** (Aragorn, LotR 5 VIII:81)

In this study only restrictive relative clauses and cleft relatives will be taken into consideration. Non-restrictive relative clauses differ considerably from the other two types in the restrictions they impose on the selection of relative pronoun forms. More to the point, however, they turn out to be of no interest in this context: as far as hobbit speech is concerned, non-restrictive relative clauses, and the choice of relative pronoun form in them, turn out to have no indexical function at all. Thus, whenever reference is made here to 'relative clauses' (without further specification), the term should be understood as referring only to restrictive relative clauses and cleft relatives.

In LotR, four different types of relative pronoun can be found in relative clauses (non-standard *what* does not occur). Table 11 shows clearly how skilfully Tolkien has used the different forms in the speech of different character groups. Relative *as* is obviously a marker of WC speech, and will be discussed further below. What is perhaps more remarkable is the fact that Ø, the most informal of the standard English forms,[13] although it is used by all the character groups, is nevertheless strongly favoured precisely by the

---

13 Cf. Quirk et al. 1985:1249, Johannesson 1982:192.

low-mimetic characters – hobbits, Breelanders and orcs.[14] Relative *that* is a neutral form, used to a great extent by all speakers. The use of *wh*-forms, finally, is primarily a characteristic of the high-mimetic characters: Dúnedain, Elves, Wizards, Rohirrim, and Gondoreans.

	as	Ø	*that*	*who/which*	Σ
WC hobbits	18 (19.4%)	37 (39.8%)	37 (39.8%)	1 (1.1%)	93
Breelanders	2 (10.5%)	5 (26.3%)	12 (63.2%)		19
Orcs	1 (4.2%)	12 (50.0%)	11 (45.8%)		24
Ents		4 (12.9%)	26 (83.9%)	1 (3.2%)	31
Dwarves		4 (7.7%)	43 (82.7%)	5 (9.6%)	52
LC hobbits		30 (21.6%)	92 (66.2%)	17 (12.2%)	139
Dúnedain		8 (5.6%)	104 (73.2%)	30 (21.1%)	142
Elves		1 (0.8%)	95 (77.9%)	26 (21.3%)	122
Wizards		15 (5.1%)	213 (72.2%)	67 (22.7%)	295
Rohirrim		2 (2.4%)	58 (69.9%)	23 (27.7%)	83
Gondoreans		4 (3.4%)	79 (68.1%)	33 (28.4%)	116

Table 11. The use of relative pronouns by different character groups in LotR.

The use of *as* as a restrictive relative pronoun has been described as typically found in "dialects and in vulgar English, in which, however, it is very common" (Poutsma 1916:984), in "vg [=vulgar] speech" (Jespersen 1927:473), and in "popular speech" (Curme and Kurath 1931:219). However, since *as* was a perfectly acceptable relative pronoun in Early Modern English (up to the early eighteenth century),[15] it does survive in a few proverbs and sayings. Two such expressions with a fossilized relative *as* occur in dialogue in LotR: Sam and Pippin both use the expression

---

14 This should not be taken as suggesting an affinity between hobbits and orcs, but rather as illustrating the fact that Tolkien stopped short of actually representing the 'brutal jargons' of the orcs, best suited for 'curses and abuse': "their language was actually more degraded and filthy than I have shown it." (LotR App. F II:4). The formal repertoire he employed to suggest the brutality of orc speech is dominated by non-standard and colloquial English forms and thus, inevitably, comes close to the representation of the speech of WC hobbits.

15 For examples, see OED s.v. **as**, †**24.a**.

handsome is as handsome does,[16] and Aragorn uses the expression *though I say it as shouldn't* at the Prancing Pony in Bree.[17] Both expressions can be found in exactly this form in modern dictionaries,[18] and the use of relative *as* thus has no indexical function here. Since these expressions are fossilized and do not represent the respective speaker's selection of relative pronoun, these three examples have not been included in the quantitative analysis of the data reported below. On the other hand, when Gaffer Gamgee uses relative *as* in the proverbial expressions *It's an ill wind as blows nobody no good* and *All's well as ends Better*,[19] he uses relative *as* creatively (along with double negation in the first and the comparative form *better* in the second example) in constructions which are consistently given with the pronoun *that* in modern reference works.[20] Consequently, these examples have been included in the quantitative data below.

With the fossilized constructions weeded out, the use of restrictive relative *as* is a clear marker of social class among hobbits, as can be seen in table 11: apart from its use by WC hobbits in the Shire (11a-c), and Breelanders (Butterbur, (11d)), it is only used once by an orc (11e). In (11c) Sam seems to be quoting Gandalf's use of relative *as*, but since Gandalf's utterance is recorded (*Not if you know anyone Ø you can trust [...]*, LotR 1 II:178) it is clear that Sam's 'quote' is actually a paraphrase; the example has consequently been counted among Sam's examples.

(11) a. But it's a pity that folk **as talk about fighting the Enemy** can't let others do their bit in their own way without interfering. (Sam, LotR 4 V:24)
b. [...] it was Drogo's weight **as sunk the boat**. (Old Noakes, LotR 1 I:15)
c. [...] he said, *no! take someone **as you can trust***. (Sam, LotR 1 V:74)

---

16 LotR 4 V:134 (Sam), 1 IX:83 (Pippin).
17 LotR 1 IX:56.
18 LDEI s.v. **HANDSOME**; OED s.v. **handsome B.** *adv.*, s.v. **say B.2.b.** *Proverbial saying.*
19 LotR 6 IX:9. This applies, of course, also to Farmer Maggot's *All's well as ends well* (LotR 1 IV:121).
20 LDEI s.v. **WELL**, s.v. **WIND**; OED s.v. **wind** sb. **16.a.**

d. If you recollect Bill Ferny and the horsethieving; his pony **as you bought**, well, it's here. (Butterbur, LotR 6 VII:53)
e. [...] there's some one loose hereabouts **as is more dangerous** [...] (Gorbag, LotR 4 X:99)

At this point it is necessary to consider whether the observed differences between the speaker categories presented in table 11 above are real or simply due to an accidental imbalance in the investigated material. The selection of relative pronoun is notoriously sensitive to different syntactic environments in which the relative pronoun occurs; thus, the different forms of the relative pronoun have different probabilities of occurrence in different environments. For example, if the subject of the relative clause is a personal pronoun (*the house Ø he built*) zero is much more common than if the subject is a noun or proper name (*the house that Jack built*); if the relative pronoun is the subject of the relative clause, the zero form is highly unlikely. Thus the observed differences might simply be due to an uneven distribution of syntactic environments over the examples produced by the different speaker categories; this would, of course, reduce the effectiveness of the pronoun forms as linguistic indices.

To check for the possible influence of different syntactic environments, four reasonably well-represented environments were selected for closer study, namely the four possible combinations of personal or non-personal antecedent with a relative pronoun in subject or object function in a restrictive relative clause. Table 12 shows the pronoun selection made by four speaker groups (WC hobbits, orcs, Rohirrim, and Gondoreans) in each of these environments. Although the distribution of the relative pronoun forms differs with the syntactic environments, we can still observe clear differences between most of the speaker categories regardless of syntactic environment (Rohirrim and Gondoreans remain almost indistinguishable, just as in table 11). It seems reasonable to conclude, then, that the observed differences between the speaker categories (table 11) really reflect the indexical function of the different forms of the relative pronoun.

Environment: RPS					
	as	Ø	that	who/which	Σ
WC hobbits	10 (43.5%)		13 (56.5%)		23
Orcs	1 (33.3%)		2 (66.7%)		3
Rohirrim			10 (41.7%)	14 (58.3%)	24
Gondoreans			14 (41.2%)	20 (58.8%)	34
Environment: RNS					
	as	Ø	that	who/which	Σ
WC hobbits	3 (23.1%)		10 (76.9%)		13
Orcs			3		3
Rohirrim			23 (95.8%)	1 (4.2%)	24
Gondoreans			25		25
Environment: RPO					
	as	Ø	that	who/which	Σ
WC hobbits	1 (33.3%)	2 (66.7%)			3
Orcs		1			1
Rohirrim		1 (25.0%)	2 (50.0%)	1 (25.0%)	4
Gondoreans			6 (60.0%)	4 (40.0%)	10
Environment: RNO					
	as	Ø	that	who/which	Σ
WC hobbits		24 (70.6%)	9 (26.5%)	1 (2.9%)	34
Orcs		9 (60.0%)	6 (40.0%)		15
Rohirrim		1 (4.0%)	20 (80.0%)	4 (16.0%)	25
Gondoreans		4 (14.3%)	21 (75.0%)	3 (10.7%)	28

Table 12. The use of relative pronouns by four speaker categories in four syntactic environments in LotR.
R = restrictive clause, P = personal antecedent, N = non-personal antecedent, S = subject function, O = object function.

Another topic of interest is the distribution of different forms over individual speakers. Table 13 below shows the relevant data for a few selected speakers (chiefly hobbits). As we can see, LC hobbits in the Shire never use restrictive relative *as*; instead, the use of restrictive relative *wh*-pronouns seems to function as a positive marker of LC speech. If this interpretation of the status of *wh*-relatives is correct, then Farmer Cotton straddles the WC-LC boundary in an interesting way, since he is the only hobbit (indeed, the only character in LotR) to use both relative *as* (outside fossilized expressions) and a *wh*-relative. This may be taken as a sign of so-called linguistic insecurity (cf. Labov 1972a:132-133): Cotton seeks to 'improve' his speech by using a 'better' form than the usual WC variant. Even so he remains very markedly a typical WC speaker: in addition to actually using relative *as* on one occasion, he also uses most of the other WC characteristics in his speech. Such linguistic insecurity is said to be typical of "the second-highest status group" (Labov 1972b:287), a description which seems to fit Farmer Cotton well, since he obviously belongs to the upper stratum of the working class in Bywater ("He's the chief person round here [...]", Merry, LotR 6 VIII:108). Thus the two syntactic variants together function as a symptom: they indicate Farmer Cotton's insecurity with respect to his speech, his (maybe subconscious) wish to speak like an LC hobbit, at the same time as he is unable to get away from his WC background.

	as	Ø	*that*	*who/which*
*Robin Smallburrow	2 (66.7%)		1 (33.3%)	
*Old Noakes	1 (50.0%)		1 (50.0%)	
*Gaffer Gamgee	2 (33.3%)	2 (33.3%)	2 (33.3%)	
Gorbag	1 (33.3%)	1 (33.3%)	1 (33.3%)	
*Farmer Cotton	1 (20.0%)	1 (20.0%)	2 (40.0%)	1 (20.0%)
*Sam Gamgee	11 (17.5%)	27 (42.9%)	25 (39.7%)	
*Farmer Maggot	1 (14.3%)	4 (57.1%)	2 (28.6%)	
‡Butterbur	2 (11.8%)	4 (23.5%)	11 (64.7%)	
†Fatty Bolger		1		
‡Gatekeeper, Bree		1		
*Tom Cotton Jr.		1		
Shagrat		3 (75.0%)	1 (25.0%)	
Uglúk		3 (50.0%)	3 (50.0%)	
Small orc		1 (50.0%)	1 (50.0%)	
*Ted Sandyman		1 (50.0%)	1 (50.0%)	
Grishnákh		3 (42.9%)	4 (57.1%)	
†Bilbo		2 (33.3%)	4 (66.7%)	
*Tookland messenger		1 (33.3%)	2 (66.7%)	
‡Bree hobbits (unid.)			1	
*Sandyman Sr.			1	
Treebeard		4 (13.3%)	25 (83.3%)	1 (3.3%)

Table 13. The use of relative pronouns by selected characters in LotR.
(* = WC Shire hobbit, † = LC hobbit, ‡ = Breelander)

	as	Ø	*that*	*who/which*
†Frodo		14 (20.0%)	50 (71.4%)	6 (8.6%)
Gimli		4 (8.7%)	37 (80.4%)	5 (10.9%)
†Pippin		5 (20.0%)	17 (68.0%)	3 (12.0%)
Beregond			14 (87.5%)	2 (12.5%)
Legolas		1 (2.7%)	31 (83.8%)	5 (13.5%)
Tom Bombadil			6 (85.7%)	1 (14.3%)
Boromir		1 (5.0%)	16 (80.0%)	3 (15.0%)
Galadriel			18 (81.8%)	4 (18.2%)
Éomer		1 (4.8%)	16 (76.2%)	4 (19.0%)
Aragorn		8 (5.7%)	102 (72.9%)	30 (21.4%)
Gandalf		15 (5.5%)	199 (72.6%)	60 (21.9%)
†Merry		8 (22.2%)	20 (55.6%)	8 (22.2%)
Elrond			19 (70.4%)	8 (29.6%)
Théoden			18 (66.7%)	9 (33.3%)
Saruman			9 (64.3%)	5 (35.7%)
Denethor		1 (6.3%)	9 (56.3%)	6 (37.5%)
Éowyn			6 (60.0%)	4 (40.0%)
Faramir		2 (4.5%)	24 (54.5%)	18 (40.9%)
Wormtongue			4 (57.1%)	3 (42.9%)
Arwen			1 (50.0%)	1 (50.0%)
Herb-master			1 (33.3%)	2 (66.7%)
Hirgon				1
Erestor				1
Erkenbrand				1
Elfhelm				1

Table 13. The use of relative pronouns by selected characters in LotR (cont.).
(* = WC Shire hobbit, † = LC hobbit, ‡ = Breelander)

2.6 Phonological reduction

2.6.1 Consonant deletion

In rapid colloquial speech it is not unusual for unstressed words to be phonologically reduced – vowels tend towards schwa (the vowel [ə]), consonants tend to be lost altogether. The loss of consonants is easier to represent in writing than vowel reduction. In LotR a small number of such forms occur, all with a clear indexical function.

The most frequently occurring form with a deleted consonant is *o'* (for *of*), as shown in (12). This form is used by a small number of WC hobbits and, from Bree, Barliman Butterbur, as is shown in table 14. The table shows only data for WC hobbits and Breelanders, since no other character groups use the form *o'*.[21]

(12) a. It takes a lot **o'** believing. (Gaffer Gamgee, LotR 6 VIII:173)
    b. What's *The Pony* to him, or mugs **o'** beer? (Butterbur, LotR 6 VII:44)

	of	*o'*
Tom Cotton/Ruffians		1
Ted Sandyman	2 (50.0%)	2 (50.0%)
Gaffer Gamgee	3 (60.0%)	2 (40.0%)
WC hobbits (unid.)	3 (75.0%)	1 (25.0%)
Farmer Cotton	42 (84.0%)	8 (16.0%)
Hob Hayward	6 (85.7%)	1 (14.3%)
Butterbur	34 (91.9%)	3 (8.1%)
Sam Gamgee	65 (94.2%)	4 (5.8%)
Farmer Maggot	8	
Robin Smallburrow	5	
Stranger	4	
Tom Cotton Jr.	3	
Shirriff	2	
Butterbur/Gandalf	1	
Daddy Twofoot	1	
Gandalf/Butterbur	1	
Gandalf/Gaffer	1	
Mrs. Maggot	1	
Nob	1	
Old Noakes	1	
Rose Cotton	1	
Sam/Gaffer	1	

Table 14. The use of the variants *of/o'* by Shire hobbits and Breelanders.

---

21 It should perhaps be pointed out that the form *o'* is not used at all in LotR 1-3. The first examples occur in LotR 4 IV, where Sam uses the form three times in rapid succession (*out o' my sight* 4 IV:38, *the time o' the year* 4 IV:42, *and a brace o' young coneys* 4 IV:52); the majority of the examples occur in LotR 6.

A slightly more widespread form of consonant deletion is found in the form *'em* for *them*, as illustrated in (13).[22] Apart from being used by WC hobbits, it is also used by Orcs and the Ruffian leader in LotR 6 VIII (table 15).

(13) a. I caught **'em** trespassing [...] and nearly set my dogs on **'em**. (Farmer Maggot, LotR 1 IV: 120)

b. Cobwebs! But what a spider! Have at **'em**, down with **'em**! (Sam, LotR 4 IX:40)

	them	*'em*
Farmer Maggot		3
Farmer Cotton	6 (60.0%)	4 (40.0%)
Robin Smallburrow	2 (66.7%)	1 (33.3%)
Sam Gamgee	20 (80.0%)	5 (20.0%)
Gaffer Gamgee	1	
Ted Sandyman	3	
Tookland messenger	1	
Σ WC hobbits	33 (71.7%)	13 (28.3%)
Butterbur	5	
Nob	1	
Σ Breelanders	6	
Gorbag		2
Shagrat		2
Uglúk		2
Grishnákh	2	
Small orc	2	
Big orc	1	
Σ Orcs	5 (45.5%)	6 (54.5%)
Ruffian leader	2 (50.0%)	2 (50.0%)

Table 15. The use of the variants *them/'em* by WC hobbits, Breelanders, orcs, and the ruffian leader.

The form *'ee* (for *ye*) can also be described in terms of consonant deletion (loss of initial glide). In the Survey of English Dialects the form is recorded all over south-western England (including Oxfordshire; cf. Orton

---

[22] Historically speaking, *'em* does not represent *them* but *hem*, the Old English dative form of the third person plural personal pronoun.

and Wakelin 1968:962-964, 1107-1110, 1122-1131; Orton and Barry 1971:888-890, 1025-1027, 1039-1048). Early in this century, Poutsma (1916:720) described it as being "used only by the vulgar". In LotR, its use is confined to the hardcore WC speakers Gaffer Gamgee, Sam Gamgee (once each) and Ted Sandyman (twice), as illustrated in (14).

(14) a. Yes, sold out and gone, I **tell'ee**. (Gaffer Gamgee, LotR 1 III:37)
 b. **Thank'ee** indeed, Mr. Cotton. (Sam, LotR 6 VIII:165)
 c. Don't **'ee** like it, Sam? (Ted Sandyman, LotR 6 VIII:205)

2.6.2 Vowel deletion

One case of vowel deletion also deserves being taken into account. This involves the deletion of the vowel in the pronoun *it* when it occurs in the combinations *it is/it was*, resulting in the forms *'tis/'twas*. In LotR, these forms are used primarily by Gondorean speakers, but also by Sam Gamgee, as shown in (15) (cf. also table 16). The explanation of this seemingly disparate constellation of speakers sharing a linguistic feature is to be found in the status of the forms *'tis/'twas* in the English language, past and present.

(15) a. [...] few of old came thence unchanged, **'tis** said. (Faramir, LotR 4 V:41)
 b. **'Twas** like a shadow on the ground [...] Perhaps under the shadow of the Unnamed some of the beasts of Mirkwood are wandering hither to our woods. They have black squirrels there, **'tis** said. (Anborn, LotR 4 V:93)
 c. Swertings we call 'em in our tales, and they ride on Oliphaunts, **'tis** said, when they fight. [...] Maybe there ain't no such a beast. (Sam, LotR 4 V:93)
 d. **'Twas** the eyes as made me sit up, so to speak. (Sam, LotR 2 IX:18)

During the seventeenth and eighteenth centuries, *'tis/'twas* were perfectly acceptable forms in written standard English (cf. Barber 1976:205), which is the reason why they can be used in the speech of the Gondoreans to indicate a remote and dignified culture. In modern English, on the other hand, these forms are not used in the standard language, but can be found in non-standard regional dialects (cf. OED s.v. **'tis**). For this reason they are wholly appropriate as indicators of working-class speech when they are used by Sam Gamgee.

It is not really as strange as it may seem at first glance that the same forms should be capable of being used with two so widely different functions. This is possible because the forms do not occur in isolation, but together with other forms with the same function. In the speech of the Gondoreans, *'tis/'twas* co-occur with other archaic forms (e.g. *thence, hither*), whereas in Sam's speech they co-occur with a host of other non-standard variants (in (15c-d) we find *'em, ain't*, double negation, and relative *as*). Thus the context in both cases helps determine the function of the forms *'tis/'twas*.

	'tis/'twas
Anborn	3
Faramir	3
Damrod	2
Ioreth	2
Gondorean (unid.)	1
Sam Gamgee	2

Table 16. The use of the contracted forms *'tis/'twas* in LotR.

3 THE LINGUISTIC SITUATION IN THE SHIRE AND BREE

The time has now come to give an integrated picture of the linguistic situation in the Shire and Bree on the basis of the data discussed above. One syntactic variant (*'ll not*) seems to function as a regional group-identifying index (section 2.4.2), thus bearing witness to dialectal differences between different parts of the Shire, and between the Shire and Bree. Another variant (finite *be*, section 2.2) is apparently best interpreted as an age-related form, used only by old speakers in the Shire. But what is the relationship between the other non-standard forms used?

The original hypothesis for this study was that it should be possible to identify systematic differences between LC and WC speech in the selection of syntactic variants, with WC speech characterized by the use of non-standard English variants. That hypothesis was certainly supported by the linguistic data from this investigation; we can, however, carry the analysis one step further. It turns out that for a number of reasonably well-documented speakers these variants can be represented as forming an implicational hierarchy (cf. Hudson 1980:184-188). The theory of implicational hierarchy predicts the existence of an ordered hierarchy of intermediate language varieties between two extreme (but related) varieties; it was originally developed to account for the linguistic situation in communities with a number of intermediate varieties (mesolects) between a dominant language (the acrolect, or high variety), e.g. English, and a creole (the basilect, or low variety) based on the acrolect. In the case of the Shire, the acrolect would be 'pure' LC speech, and the basilect 'pure' WC speech.

Just as the mesolects can be described as forming a hierarchy between the acrolect and the basilect, the linguistic variants which have an indexical function within this hierarchy can be described as being more or less strongly marked for 'non-acrolectal' status. A more strongly marked variant is one whose use is restricted to mesolects closer to the basilect.

An implicational hierarchy is made up of the relevant linguistic variants that are used in the speech community, from the most basilectal to the most acrolectal variants. By definition, the presence of a more strongly marked variant in the speech of an individual implies the presence of all the less strongly marked variants in the speech of that individual. Individual speakers can be ranked on a so-called implicational scale, depending on how many of the relevant variants they use. Figure 2 below presents such an implicational scale for a number of individual speakers from the Shire and Bree.

	AG	AS	O'	DN	EM	LN	AN	EE	PF	PG	OU	'T	
LC speakers	−	−	−	−	−	−	−	−	−	−	−	−	0
Old Noakes	•	+	−	−	−	−	−	−	−	−	−	−	2 (1)
Tom Cotton Jr.	+	•	+	−	−	−	−	−	−	−	−	−	3 (2)
Gatekeeper	•	•	•	+	−	−	−	−	−	−	−	−	4 (1)
Hob Hayward	+	•	+	+	−	−	−	−	−	−	−	−	4 (3)
Robin Smallburrow	+	+	•	•	+	−	−	−	−	−	−	−	5 (3)
Farmer Maggot	+	+	•	•	+	+	−	−	−	−	−	−	6 (4)
Butterbur	+	+	+	+	•	+	−	−	−	−	−	−	6 (5)
Ted Sandyman	+	•	+	•	•	•	+	+	−	−	−	−	8 (4)
Farmer Cotton	+	+	+	+	+	+	•	•	+	+	−	−	10 (8)
Gaffer Gamgee	+	+	+	+	•	•	+	+	+	•	+	−	11 (8)
Sam Gamgee	+	+	+	+	+	+	+	+	+	+	+	+	12
	11 (9)	11 (7)	10 (7)	9 (6)	7 (4)	6 (4)	4 (3)	4 (3)	3	3 (2)	2	1	

Figure 2. An implicational scale for selected speakers from the Shire and Bree.[23]

AG = non-standard subject–verb agreement, AS = relative *as*, O' = *of* realized as *o'*, DN = double negation, EM = *'em*, LN = *'ll not*, AN = *ain't*, EE = *ye* realized as *'ee*, PF = prefixed perfect, PG = prefixed progressive, OU = *ought to* with *do*-periphrasis, 'T = *'tis/'twas*. + = attested variants, − = non-attested variants, • = predicted, non-attested variants.

One advantage of the implicational scale analysis should be immediately obvious: it provides a rationale for predicting the use of non-attested

---

23 The implicational scale has been constructed in accordance with the following criteria:
1. Features (variants) are first ordered according to the number of speakers using the feature (i.e. the number of +-signs for each feature);
2. Speakers are next ordered according to the position of the rightmost +-sign for each speaker;
3. If two speakers have the rightmost +-sign in the same position, the internal ordering of these speakers is determined by the number of +-signs for each speaker;
4. If two features have an equal number of +-signs (which means their internal ordering cannot be determined by criterion 1), the internal ordering of the features which agrees best with criteria 2 and 3 is seleceted (this puts AS before O');
5. If the internal ordering of two features cannot be determined by criteria 1 and 4, the internal ordering which minimizes the number of predicted occurrences is selected (this puts EM before LN).
This leaves only the internal ordering of AN and EE indeterminate.

variants (indicated by • in figure 2) implied by other variants which actually occur in the text. This is most strikingly the case with the nameless gatekeeper at the Brandywine Bridge, whose few utterances (LotR 6 VIII:15) yield one instance of double negation, thus permitting us to predict his use of three other variants.

The implicational scale can furthermore be interpreted as showing to what extent the individual speakers identify themselves with the working class in their speech. Non-standard agreement and relative *as* are clearly the most stable markers of WC speech, since they are used by (or predicted for) all the speakers concerned. By contrast, the other non-standard variants can be regarded as symptoms indicating various degrees of identification, or solidarity, with the working class. Sam Gamgee then emerges – not unexpectedly – as the speaker who exhibits the strongest solidarity with the working class, closely followed by his father, Gaffer Gamgee.[24]

Although the implicational scale interpretation of the data is attractive, it must be remembered that it is by no means the only possible interpretation. For one thing, it presupposes a stable, unchanging language system, in which the presence or absence of a variant in an individual WC hobbit's speech is determined solely by the internal relationships between the variants and the speaker's class solidarity. If, instead, we allow for the possibility of language change in progress in hobbit speech, and treat the speaker's age and place of origin as determining factors, we can interpret the data in a different way.

As was pointed out in section 2.2 above, the use of finite BE is presumably best interpreted as an age-related phenomenon, a variant that has been lost in the speech of younger WC hobbits. In section 2.3.2 it was argued that the use of *'ll not* was regionally related, with higher frequencies

---

[24] One possible source of error that has to be kept in mind is the fact that there is a very strong correlation between the volume of speech recorded for each WC speaker and the number of non-standard features used by that speaker. Ideally, all the informants should be equally represented in the material; since the input data for this study are determined by the dialogue in LotR, however, there is nothing that can be done to redress the imbalance between the speakers in this respect.

of occurrence in the eastern parts of the Shire and in Bree. Similarly, as a look at figure 2 will show, it could well be the case that the prefixed participle forms are recessive variants, surviving only in a relict area in the central parts of the Shire (including the Hobbiton/Bywater area), since they are only used by the Gamgees and Farmer Cotton among the WC speakers.[25] It may be significant that the only other character to use a prefixed participle is Tom Bombadil, whose great age would certainly justify any old-fashioned features in his speech (note that he also uses finite BE).

The use of *ain't*, *'ee*, *ought to* with *do*-periphrasis, and *'tis/'twas* also seems to be regionally restricted, since these forms are only attested from the same area (Hobbiton/Bywater). If we adopt this interpretation, then Farmer Maggot's and Butterbur's speech would also be maximally marked for working class membership (like Sam's), since the six rightmost variants in figure 2 would not be available in the dialects of their regions (the Marish and Bree, respectively). An interpretation of prefixed participles and *'ee* as representing regionally restricted, receding variants is certainly consistent with their status in the primary world (cf. Trudgill 1978:15); as regards *ain't*, it was regionally restricted in England in the early part of this century (Orton et al. 1978, Maps M9-M15), even though its use may be more widespread now as a result of American influence.

In the final analysis, then, it turns out that for a number of non-standard variants two interpretations are possible: either their use is sociologically determined (the implicational hierarchy interpretation), and in the speech of the individual character they function as symptoms, indicating the speaker's degree of solidarity with the working class, or their use is regionally and/or diachronically determined (the 'ongoing change' interpretation), and in the speech of the individual character they function as regional and/or age-related group-identifying indices. In order to narrow down the possibilities further, it would be necessary to carry out more 'fieldwork' than the available data in LotR allow us to do; thus, the choice between the rival

---

25 For a comment on Lobelia Sackville-Baggins' use of this WC feature, see sections 2.2 and 2.4.1. The prefixed participles seem to be more tenacious (within their limited area of distribution) than finite BE, since they are used by a young speaker such as Sam Gamgee.

interpretations will be a subjective matter for the individual reader. But whichever interpretation we choose, the presence of these non-standard variants in dialogue in LotR contributes to the characterization of a linguistically diversified speech community in which the individual speaker finds his or her place (sociolinguistically speaking) as the result of continuous linguistic choices.

4 CONCLUSION

J.R.R. Tolkien, in his essay »On Fairy-Stories«, sees the role of the author as that of a sub-creator:

> He makes a Secondary World which your mind can enter. Inside it, what he relates is 'true': it accords with the laws of that world. [...] To make a Secondary World [...] will probably require labour and thought, and will certainly demand a special skill, a kind of elvish craft.
> (Tolkien 1938/39:36 & 46).

Such an 'elvish craft' will, needless to say, manifest itself in many different ways. This paper has explored one of its aspects, namely Tolkien's use of non-standard English in the speech of various characters in *The Lord of the Rings*. By his use of non-standard English forms and constructions Tolkien managed to sub-create a speech community in which social stratification can be seen reflected in the speech of the members of this community. In addition, we can find evidence of linguistic accommodation to other speakers, linguistic insecurity, dialect variation, and language change.[26] The

---

26 Unfortunately there is no evidence of gender-related linguistic variation among hobbits, for the simple reason that almost no female hobbit speech is recorded in LotR. The only exceptions are a few utterances by Lobelia Sackville-Baggins (LC, LotR 1 I:149-155, 1 III:32), Mrs. Maggot (WC, LotR 1 IV:105), Rose Cotton and her mother (WC, LotR 6 VIII:124-129), in which no non-standard variants occur (see, however, the discussion of Tom Cotton Jr.'s report of Lobelia's exchange with the ruffians, sections 2.2 and 2.4.1 above). It may be tempting to see this as an indication that female hobbits are more status-conscious than male hobbits and thus less prone to use non-standard variants; again, such a situation would reflect a general trend in the English-speaking world (cf. Trudgill 1974:84-102).

representation of speech in *The Lord of the Rings* accords not only with the laws of the Secondary World, but with what is known about linguistic variation in our primary world as well.

REFERENCES

BARBER, Charles. 1976. *Early Modern English.* London: André Deutsch.

CARPENTER, Humphrey (ed., with the assistance of Christopher Tolkien). 1981. *The Letters of J.R.R. Tolkien.* London: George Allen and Unwin. Rpt. 1995 (HarperCollins).

CHRISTIE, Agatha. 1980. *Hickory Dickory Dock.* London: Fontana Paperbacks.

CRAWFORD, Edward. 1985. *Some Light on Middle-earth.* Pinner, Middx.: The Tolkien Society.

CURME, C.O. and Hans KURATH. 1931. *A Grammar of the English Language. Vol. III. Syntax.* Boston, Mass.: D.C. Heath & Co.

GILES, Howard and Philip M. SMITH. 1979. »Accommodation Theory: Optimal Levels of Convergence.« In: Howard Giles and Robert St. Clair (eds.). 1979. *Language and Social Psychology.* Oxford: Blackwells, 45-65.

JESPERSEN, Otto. 1927. *A Modern English Grammar.* Part III. Syntax. Second volume. Heidelberg: Carl Winters Universitätsbuchhandlung.

– – –. 1940. *A Modern English Grammar.* Part V. Syntax. Fourth volume. Copenhagen: Munksgaard.

JOHANNESSON, Nils-Lennart. 1982. »On the use of postmodification in English noun phrases.« In: Waldemar Gutwinski and Grace Jolly (eds.). 1982. *The Eighth LACUS Forum 1981.* Columbia, S.C.: Hornbeam Press, 187-195.

KILBY, Clyde S. 1976. *Tolkien & The Silmarillion.* Wheaton, Ill.: Harold Shaw.

LABOV, William. 1972a. *Sociolinguistic Patterns.* Philadelphia, Pa.: University of Philadelphia Press.

– – –. 1972b. »The Study of Language in its Social Context.« In: Pier Paolo Giglioli (ed.). 1972. *Language and Social Context.* Harmondsworth: Penguin Books, 283-307.

LDEI = *Longman Dictionary of English Idioms.* 1985. London: Longman.

OED = *The Oxford English Dictionary.* 2nd ed., 1989. Oxford: OUP.

ORTON, Harold and Michael BARRY (eds.). 1969-71. *Survey of English Dialects: The Basic Material.* Vol. 2. The West Midland Counties. Leeds: E.J. Arnold.

ORTON, Harold and Wilfrid J. HALLIDAY (eds.). 1963. *The Survey of English Dialects. Basic Material.* Vol. 1. The Six Northern Counties and the Isle of Man. Part 3. Leeds: E.J. Arnold.

ORTON, Harold and Martyn F. WAKELIN (eds.). 1968. *The Survey of English Dialects. Basic Material.* Vol. 4. The Southern Counties. Part 3. Leeds: E.J. Arnold.

ORTON, Harold, Stewart SANDERSON and John WIDDOWSON. 1978. *The Linguistic Atlas of England*. London: Croom Helm.

PARTRIDGE, Eric. 1947. *Usage and Abusage: A Guide to Good English*. London: Hamish Hamilton.

POUTSMA, H. 1916. *A Grammar of Late Modern English*. Part II. The Parts of Speech. Section I, B. Pronouns and Numerals. Groningen: P. Noordhoff.

QUIRK, Randolph, Sidney GREENBAUM, Geoffrey LEECH and Jan SVARTVIK. 1985. *A Comprehensive Grammar of English*. London: Longman.

TOLKIEN, J.R.R. 1938/39. »On Fairy-Stories.« Reprinted 1988 in *Tree and Leaf*. London: Grafton.

TRUDGILL, Peter. 1974. *Sociolinguistics. An Introduction.* Harmondsworth: Penguin Books.

– – – (ed.). 1978. *Sociolinguistic Patterns in British English*. London: Edward Arnold.

From Bag End to Lórien: the Creation of a Literary World

THOMAS HONEGGER

Summary

Tolkien's fictional world is not merely the backdrop for the unfolding plot, but rather a 'protagonist' in its own right. The analysis of the places visited by the Fellowship in the first part of the narrative (from Bag End to Lothlórien) will illustrate the function of places in Tolkien's work. Their function is threefold. First, they primarily constitute his narrative universe; second, the description of the habitat of a people is an important instrument to characterise its inhabitants and supplements or even replaces a straightforward characterisation. And third, the assignment of a 'homeland' to a people implies a tacit approval. In a sense, the lack of a place of origin, of a 'home', points to a moral deficiency.

1 INTRODUCTION

"In the beginning was the Word, and the Word was with God" (John 1,1). For Tolkien, one would have to modify the biblical sentence as: "In the beginning were the Elvish tongues, and the Elvish tongues were with Tolkien." Indeed, as he himself states: "it [i.e. his creation of the Middle-earth cosmos] was primarily linguistic in inspiration and was begun in order to provide the necessary background of 'history' for Elvish tongues" (Foreword LotR:9).[1] Yet Tolkien, being a good Catholic, has never seen himself in competition with God the Creator. He positioned himself somewhere further down the hierarchy and humbly called his creative work 'sub-creation'. Also, he did not think of himself as a semi-divine 'demiurg', but rather as a chronicler of the events that took place in Middle-earth ages ago. This attitude towards his work made him a very careful and scrupulous 'architect' of Middle-earth, who cared greatly about the internal coherence of his world. This, in combination with the sheer bulk of material

---

1 All references to *The Lord of the Rings* (henceforth LotR) are to the centenary one volume edition (based on the one volume edition of 1968) published by Grafton 1992.

accumulated, had the effect that today Middle-earth has attained an independent existence, i.e. an existence outside the literary works of Tolkien. Publications like Fonstad's *The Atlas of Middle-earth*, Day's various encyclopaedic works on Middle-earth, and the 'continued subcreation' by other authors of fiction have substantially contributed to this development.

Also, during the last few decades a wealth of source- and background-material to Tolkien's work has been made available to the general public. Tolkien's religious and mythological concepts for his world have been accessible since the posthumous publication of *The Silmarillion* in 1977, and the multi-volume series of *The History of Middle-earth* provides a plethora of source-material on Tolkien's works of fiction. Though these publications provide welcome and much needed aid for the discussion of textual problems, they nevertheless present a danger to the scholar who explores Tolkien's work, since s/he might easily get lost in the maze of textual layers and variants out of which probably not even Tolkien himself would have found an easy way out. My discussion of the use and function of the spatial dimension will therefore be limited to the works published during Tolkien's lifetime, i.e. LotR and, of lesser importance for this study, *The Hobbit*. This limitation has the advantage of providing us with an uncluttered view of the world which Tolkien presented to his contemporary readers.

Before entering the realm of Middle-earth, I first want to consider a few points which distinguish Tolkien from an 'average' author of fiction. Tolkien does not use fictional protagonists in a real world. An author who makes use of our world as the backdrop to her/his narrative inherits the symbolic dimension of a real-world site. S/he cannot ignore the accumulated historically determined meaning(s) of a place in our world. Thus, Dublin in Joyce's *Ulysses* and London in Dickens' works provide not only the background for the action but are often at least as important as the human protagonists.

Tolkien, however, does not only deal with fictional characters, but with an entire fictional world. Although Middle-earth is in some respect our world, he situates his narrative in a prehistoric as well as mythical era and thus avoids the historic predetermination of his fiction.[2] Moreover, he excludes one of the most important forces that generates symbolic meaning for places, namely religion.[3] This tacit omission might be due to the fact that he had realised that incorporating the rich yet still disordered and incomplete mythological material would put too great a strain onto the narrative.

Tolkien's stance of seeing himself as the chronicler of events long past resulted in the slow and organic growth of Middle-earth. He did not rush his world into a premature and shortlived bloom, but took care to let it develop at its own pace. He preferred to make a detour into history, and thus to add depth to his fiction, rather than to hastily cover as much ground as possible.[4] It took even God six days to create our universe, and Tolkien certainly did not want to compete with Him. This slow and unhurried development brought about the simultaneous existence of different, sometimes opposing layers of symbolic meanings. Traces of this can be seen in the change of place names. 'Minas Ithil' ('Tower of the Moon') is renamed 'Minas Morgul' ('Tower of the Wraiths') after it has fallen into the hands of Sauron (LotR:621 & 1187). The 'symbolic value' of this place has undergone a change from positive to negative. And yet, the former meaning, though covered by the new one, is still present in the minds of the protagonists. A similar development, yet without a change of name, has taken place in

---

[2] See Day (1994:15): "Central to Tolkien's creative effort was the illusion that Middle-earth was a world of archetypes that survived in the racial unconscious of the English people. All the English are and know comes from this world. All great events of English history are prefigured in archetypical form in this ancient mythic world."

[3] The religious-mythical history of Middle-earth has been in existence right from the beginning, yet was excluded from the narrative works and posthumously published in *The Silmarillion*. The only explicit reference to religious practice in LotR is the 'saying grace' by the Gondoreans in (LotR:702-703) – which struck the hobbits present as strange. On the somewhat tenuous connection between experience of space and religious experience, see Dowie (1979).

[4] On this effect of 'depth', see Shippey (1992:203): "One quality which that work has in abundance is the Beowulfian 'impression of depth', created just as in the old epic by songs and digressions like Aragorn's lay of Tinúviel, Sam Gamgee's allusions to the Silmaril and the Iron Crown, Elrond's account of Celebrimor, and dozens more."

Moria. The protagonists and also the readers experience the mines as a dark, deserted and dangerous place. However, it must not be forgotten that it has once been something like the 'Promised Land' for the dwarves, as Gimli correctly points out.

Tolkien does not only present the same place now and then, but likewise introduces a plurality of culturally determined perceptions that exist side by side. Lothlórien, for example, is not the paradisical Mallorn-grove for everybody. The Rohirrim refer to it by the not very flattering name 'Dwimordene' (LotR:536), which can be translated as 'Vale of Illusion'. For them, it is a place only vaguely known from hearsay, associated with magic and wizardry and therefore held in superstitious awe.

2 STRUCTURE

The complexity and quantity of data available forces me to limit my study to the analysis of three central aspects of Tolkien's use of space. I will only refer to the initial books of LotR to illustrate my points. The three central aspects may be formulated in thesis-form as follows:

1) Space is important in the war between Good and Evil. This conflict does not take place in an abstract and lifeless vacuum, but in a world emotionally close to the reader.

2) The habitat, or lebensraum, is used to characterise its inhabitants, as is especially obvious with the hobbits of the Shire.

3) The protagonists' relationship with space is an indicator for their moral attitude. Generally speaking, morally sound characters interact positively with their surroundings, whereas negative characters are mostly without a proper homeland and have an obvious tendency to damage or pervert their lebensraum.

Before I go on discussing these three basic aspects, it is necessary to have a closer look at the narrative as well as geographic heartpiece of Middle-earth: the Shire.

3 THE SHIRE

It is certainly not by chance that the initial idea to *The Hobbit*, and thus also to *The Lord of the Rings*, can be traced back to the – at first – enigmatic sentence "In a hole in the ground there lived a hobbit". Tolkien had scribbled it onto a sheet from an examination paper and then had first to find out what or who 'a hobbit' was. Please note that this simple sentence contains the central unknown 'hobbit'. The additional information given ('in a hole in the ground', 'lived', and 'a') enables us to deduce the following: 'hobbit' is a countable noun (indicated by the indefinite article 'a') which designates an animate (indicated by the verb 'lived') and at least partially settled being (indicated by the adverbial phrase 'in a hole in the ground'). Thus, *The Hobbit* opens with the definition of the main protagonst via his habitat – which is, later on, backed up by Tolkien's pseudo-Anglo-Saxon etymology of '*hol-bytla = hole-dweller'.

The world of LotR is in many ways the same as the one of *The Hobbit*. Yet, the predominant fairy-tale chattyness has given way to a sombre tone. Nevertheless, the (re-)entry into Middle-earth again takes place via a detailed description of the Shire. The fifteen pages of the prologue provide a detailed account of the history, geography and the social and economic situation of the Shire. No other people gets nearly as extensive a treatment by Tolkien as the hobbits. The information we get about elves and dwarves must be gathered either from the sparse hints in the narrative or from the somewhat more detailed accounts in the appendices A II and F I. Of course, one has to take into consideration that elves and dwarves should be familiar from the mythology of our primary world. The hobbits, however, are complete 'newcomers', and it is therefore necessary to provide an in-depth discussion of this loveable people.

In spite of the fact that the hobbits are not known from primary world mythology, they soon become familiar to the reader. Hobbits lack the otherworldly beauty and awesomeness of the elves, and are easier to get along with than the somewhat grumpy dwarves. Indeed, hobbits are, to some extent, 'better humans'. They mostly lack the aggressive traits found in our race and they have cultivated a homeliness alien to most human protagonists in LotR. Also, the introduction of hobbits prepares the readers for the appearance of dwarves, elves, orcs, ents and all the various exotic and mythical peoples.

Tolkien takes great pains to establish the Shire in the minds – and even more in the hearts – of the readers as their 'homeland' in Middle-earth. And it is to the Shire that we will return more than a thousand pages later. The very beginnings of both *The Hobbit* and LotR take us into the cosy and homely dwelling-hole at Bag End, and most readers feel severely tempted to put on their imaginary slippers and settle down to a piece of cake and some tea. Even an outing into the Shire does not change the reader's attitude. The smallish country inhabited by the hobbits is the very epitome of a pre-industrial idyll. The cultivated fields, the green pastures, the neat gardens and the picturesque villages charm the reader.

Nevertheless, the Shire is no utopia in the narrow sense of the meaning. There are undeniably utopian elements, but the Shire as a whole is very much 'down to earth' and real – and sometimes fairly parochial in its outlook. This becomes obvious when it is contrasted to Lothlórien. The timelessness and otherworldly seclusion of the elven-homestead is incompatible with the rustic and petit bourgeois homeliness of the hobbit homeland. Therefore, we may call the Shire 'the heart' of Middle-earth – and Lothlórien 'the soul'.

The position of the Shire within the narrative is crucial. Its detailed and extensive description, apart from making the reader welcome to Middle-earth, establishes the hobbit-homeland as the norm by which all the following landscapes and places will be measured. The fact that most of the story is told from the hobbits' point of view strengthens this effect. The 'hobbit-perspective' also makes itself felt otherwise. Thus, Shippey (1992:94-95) remarked ironically that the first stages of the journey resemble not so much a 'journey', but a sequence of comfortable homesteads that have to be left more or less hurriedly (Bag End, Crickhollow, Tom Bombadil's home, 'The Prancing Pony' and Elrond's house at Rivendell). This criticism is true to a great extent, yet it must be taken into account that the stress laid on these 'rest-stops' is in accordance with the character of the fictitious hobbit-narrator. They are, as 'hol-bytlan' (hole-dwellers), in the first place stationary beings who have a deep-rooted aversion against travelling outside the Shire. Travelling abroad belongs to the same class as adventures. Both are "[n]asty disturbing uncomfortable things! Make you late for dinner!" (Hobbit:16). Also, these 'rest-stops' often fulfil an important narrative function. At Elrond's home, for example, the foundation for the future development is laid. And last, they offer to the reader a periodical 'break' (a kind of parallel to 'comic relief') from action and suspense – something not to be underrated in a narrative of the dimension of LotR.

But let me return to the Shire itself. The most important narrative function of the hobbits' homeland is, without doubt, its archetypical value. The Shire becomes the reader's archetypical homeland, '*the* place' pure and simple. So it is '*the* Shire' (definite article), and even its landscape features such as rivers, marshes and hills are '*the* Water', '*the* Marish', and '*the* Hill', to name only a few examples. Tolkien puts into practice what he has postulated in his essay »On Fairy-Stories« (Tolkien 1938/39:70):

> If a story says, 'he climbed a hill and saw a river in the valley below', the illustrator may catch, or nearly catch, his own vision of such a scene; every hearer of the words will have his own picture, and it will be made out of all the hills and rivers and dales he has ever seen, but specially out of The Hill, The River, The Valley which were for him the first embodiment of the word.

Thus, in this part of Middle-earth at least, place-names are still identical with what they denominate. The 'paradisical' original unity of language and world seems to be intact yet.

The archetypical quality of the Shire is further stressed by the seclusion of the hobbit-homeland, far away from the world of great events. One might object that the reader, in contrast to the hobbit-protagonists, has a wider horizon right from the start – due to the survey-maps printed or added at the beginning of the book. These survey-maps, however, are later additions, drawn by Christopher Tolkien. Tolkien himself made do with rough sketches for quite some time. He needed a 'masterplan' to synchronize the events and movements of his protagonists only after the story and the various parallel plots had developed both in length and complexity. However, Tolkien himself talks about his writing process as a kind of journey (LotR:9): "[...], and I plodded on, mostly by night, till I stood at Balin's tomb in Moria. [...] It was almost a year later when I went on and so came to Lothlórien and the Great River in 1941." This comment is of relevance for our discussion, since Tolkien obviously did not get his bearings by the unfolding of the action, but by the sequence of places. He seemed to experience his creative process as a gradual opening up of geographic, historical and symbolical dimensions of Middle-earth.

The survey-map at the beginning of LotR is misleading since it has no counterpart in the narrative structure and, from a narratological point of view, it should be moved to a position further back. The reader should rather feel like Frodo studying the maps of the Shire: "He looked at maps, and wondered what lay beyond their edges: maps made in the Shire showed mostly white spaces beyond its borders." (LotR:56). It is not yet time for Frodo and his friends or for the reader to glimpse the terrors and joys of the lands beyond. They must remain, for the moment, 'terra incognita'. Meanwhile Tolkien takes great care to make the reader feel at home in the Shire. Only after having successfully established a safe 'home base' does he lead reader and protagonists into those unknown and wild parts of Middle-earth that are full of wonders and dangers. Who does not yearn, together with the hobbits on their journey, for their homely hobbit-holes and the pleasant fields of the Shire? This is because we have the opportunity to stay a while in this blessed country, to share the hobbits' love for their homeland. And it is also due to our sojourn in the Shire that we fall in love with Middle-earth as a whole. Tolkien captures the reader's heart by means of this simple yet so loveable corner of Eriador. He does not really need the idealised homestead of Rivendell nor the transcendental beauty of

Lothlórien to make us care for the fate of Middle-earth. These are nice and beautiful places in their own right, and one would certainly bemourn their disappearance. Yet, our heart remains in the hobbit-homeland and it is his love for the Shire that gives Frodo the strength to endure (LotR:76):

> I feel that as long as the Shire lies behind, safe and comfortable, I shall find wandering more bearable: I shall know that somewhere there is a firm foothold, even if my feet cannot stand there again.

Sam, too, thinks back to the Shire when he cannot find Frodo in the Tower of Cirith Ungol. The thought of his native country gives him new hope (LotR:943): "He murmured old childish tunes out of the Shire, and snatches of Mr. Bilbo's rhymes that came into his mind like fleeting glimpses of the country of his home." Indeed, the Shire is one of the 'places of power', as Gandalf points out (LotR:239): "There is power, too, of another kind [than in Rivendell or Lothlórien] in the Shire." Thus, the Shire becomes the emotional as well as the narrative basis for the ensuing description of Middle-earth – which remains incomplete and selective, in spite of the encyclopaedic concept of Tolkien's 'sub-creation'.

The first phase, i.e. the successful creation of the idyll, ends with the intrusion of the outer world. The advent of the Dark Riders and the more enjoyable meeting with the elves (LotR:92) give a taste of the events to come and start the process of widening the hitherto limited horizon.

4 FROM BAG END TO LÓRIEN

The geographic as well as the historical development of Middle-earth starts with the movement of the main hobbit protagonists towards the periphery of the Shire, i.e. from Bag End to Crickhollow, and continues beyond the border into the Old Forest, which presents an interesting contrast to the carefully cultivated and domesticated Shire.

The Old Forest

The Old Forest has remained more or less untouched by the great upheavals of Middle-earth history, thus preserving nature in its original state. Yet, it would be wrong to think of this nature as benevolent or even 'paradisical'. The Old Forest is an original wilderness, above and beyond moral categories and political alliances. Not unlike its 'genius loci', Tom Bombadil, it has always been and thus simply is! The hobbits face their first test in this wilderness (Old Man Willow) and experience the negative aspects of nature. However, the Old Forest is also the realm of 'Master' Bombadil, who not only saves the hobbits from the deadly embrace of Old Man Willow, but also, later on, from the spell of the Barrow-wight. This way the Old Forest and the adjoining Barrow Downs become the site for the initiation of the hobbits into the basically ambiguous nature of both nature (the Old Forest) and history (the barrows).

Bree

Bree, the next major stopover, functions as a point of transition between the hobbit-homeland and the wide expanse of Eriador. Though not part of the Shire proper anymore, it offers still some degree of Shire homeliness and comfort. The architecture of 'The Prancing Pony' suitably mirrors the situation in this 'bordertown' with its mixed human-hobbit population. The overall appearance of the guesthouse is that of a normal mannish inn, yet it offers several rooms that have been built into the hill, thus imitating traditional hobbit-architecture.

Rivendell

The development of the narrative space of Middle-earth finds its temporary climax at Rivendell, in the Last Homely House east of the Sea (LotR:241). Bilbo once characterised Elrond's home as follows (LotR:241):

> 'That house [is ...] a perfect house, whether you like food or sleep, or story-telling or singing, or just sitting and thinking best, or a pleasant mixture of them all'. Merely to be there was a cure for weariness, fear, and sadness.

Architecture (in the widest sense of the word) at its best! Of the rooms described, the Hall of Fire is of special interest to us (LotR:246ff.). It is here that elves, half-elves (Elrond), men (Aragorn), hobbits (Bilbo) and, at least temporarily, also dwarves (Gimli) assemble to listen to stories and songs. It is a place where the various free peoples from all over Middle-earth harmoniously mingle with each other, irrespective of race and status. The homely Hall of Fire has a more official counterpart in the room where the Council of Elrond meets (LotR:256ff.). There the representatives of the free peoples gather to talk business and to discuss their strategy in the upcoming confrontation with the Dark Lord. For the time of the meeting, Elrond's 'Last Homely House east of the Sea' becomes the 'omphalos', the symbolic centre of Middle-earth.

Rivendell is a world apart, not unlike the Shire. Yet, whereas the homeland of the hobbits has become a provincial backwater, untouched by the great upheavals of history because it is too unimportant, Rivendell is one of the two places protected by the power of the Elven-rings. The home of Elrond is a place of culture and learning – on a level which surpasses the homely yet humble achievements of the hobbits by far. One has only to place the songs sung in the Hall of Fire next to Frodo's delightful yet nonsensical ballad of the 'Man in the Moon' – performed in 'The Prancing Pony' – and the contrast becomes obvious. The superior civilisatory achievement of the elves goes hand in hand with a pronounced tendency towards a certain 'otherworldliness'. We have been very well informed about the economic and agricultural basis of the Shire, yet we are given no hint as to how the inhabitants of Rivendell make a living. They eat and drink, and not too bad at that, but they are never shown at cultivating the land or hunting. However, the reader does happily without this kind of information. We are not interested in the import and export statistics of Rivendell, nor how Elrond manages his natural resources. Rivendell and the 'Last Homely House east of the Sea' fulfil a different narrative function than the Shire, where the economic data made sense. Elrond's home is a place where the sometimes hurried narrative comes to a rest, where issues raised but not answered during the first part are dealt with. At the same time we take a look into the future. The groundwork for the development to come is laid, plans are made, and the general framework for the confrontation is established. This way the often somewhat confusing and seemingly unconnected individual strands of the action are incorporated into a holistic vision of events.

Lothlórien

The next and last 'utopian' place to be visited by the Fellowship of the Ring is Lothlórien. It is presented as a primarily mythical place where even time seems to follow different laws.[5] And it has an even greater tendency towards 'otherworldliness' than Rivendell. Elrond's home has been open to travellers from all over Middle-earth. Lothlórien, however, is a place under siege which has closed its borders to outsiders. Therefore, the welcome of the Fellowship of the Ring is less warm than in Rivendell. While Lothlórien closes itself against the menacing world outside, it remains ever so open to the 'transcendental'. This becomes visible in the fact that nearly all the places are open towards the sky. The airy atmosphere of Lórien, where the majority of the interactions takes place under the open sky and where private rooms are not mentioned, is the transcendental counterpart to the closely defined homeliness of a hobbit-hole in the Shire. In this sense, Lothlórien and the Shire occupy two extreme positions on a scale where Rivendell, incorporating elements of both hobbit-homeliness and elven-otherworldiness, is to be placed somewhere in the middle. The Shire can be seen as an 'earthly paradise', a kind of Cockaigne, whereas Lothlórien comes close to our ideas of 'locus amoenus' and 'transcendental paradise'. This contrast, as encountered in the narrative, can be further substantiated by means of a comparison of two of Tolkien's pictures, namely his 'The Hall at Bag End, Residence of B. Baggins Esquire' (Chr. Tolkien 1979:No.

---

5   The protagonists thought that they had "remained some days in Lothlórien, so far as they could tell or remember" (LotR:377). In reality, however, they stayed an entire month (16 January till 16 February; cf. Appendix B, LotR:1129).

20) and 'The Forest of Lothlórien in Spring' (Chr. Tolkien 1979:No. 25).[6] The first picture shows the homely yet narrowly limited space of a hobbit-hole with the similarly neat and defined landscape of the Shire in the background. The second picture, however, presents no particular place, but an airy glade in a forest filled with sunlight, evoking a feeling of sheltered openness.

Lothlórien, and more exactly the City of Trees, Caras Galadhon, are even less characterised economically than Rivendell. Sam, to his astonishment, gets to know at the end of their stay that the elves are expert rope-makers (LotR:391f.). This astonishment is understandable since we never see elves at work. The mood of Caras Galadhon is not very inducive to a socio-economic analysis. It would be quite out of place and to some extent damaging to the 'otherworldliness' of the elves to see them doing something as trivial as manufacturing rope. Tolkien also refrains from dividing the space of the city into private living-space, public space, or working space. He prefers to keep the picture of Caras Galadhon unfocussed, undefined and vague. The omission of elements that would jar with the idealized image of the elven city ensures that it is perceived all the more as an otherworldly paradise.

---

6 It is telling that nearly all of Tolkien's picture show landscapes or places, and not primarily people.

Space ...

Lothlórien is the last place visited by the Fellowship before it breaks up. The development so far can be summarized as follows:

The Shire	(Old Forest)	Bree	Rivendell	(Moria)	Lórien
Hobbits	Nature / Old Man Willow / Tom Bombadil & Goldberry	Hobbits / Humans	(Half-) Elves / Humans / Hobbits / (Dwarves)	originally Dwarves, now Orcs & Balrog	Elves
on / in the ground	- - -	on the ground	on the ground	under ground: 'in their halls of stone' (LotR:64)	above ground: 'under the sky' (LotR:64)
secluded & remote 'petit bourgeois' idyll	untamed nature	interface between The Shire and the 'wide world'	idyll open to the world	former 'promised land' of the Dwarves, now 'under-world'	transcendental / idealised idyll

We start out from an orderly and homely hobbit hole in the Shire with its limited horizon, pass through the Old Forest on the way to Bree, which, with its mixed population of hobbits and men, functions as the gate to the wider world of Eriador. Elrond's home in Rivendell symbolises a similar point of fusion and transition, yet this time on a higher level. The Last Homely House east of the Sea is not only the home of elves, but also of men, hobbits and, temporarily, dwarves. It thus presents a harmonious side by side of the free peoples. The next station on the journey are the deserted mines of Moria. The visit to the abandoned city allows the reader one of the rare glimpses into the habitat of dwarves. At the same time, however, the encounter with the Balrog gives a hint to the dangers that lie hidden in the deepest depths of Middle-earth. Lothlórien, then, after the trial of Moria, offers peace and shelter and concludes the series of 'utopian places' that was begun with the Shire.

... and Time

The establishment of the historical or 'temporal' dimension of Middle-earth occurs parallel to its spatial development. The Shire is, relatively speaking, a very recent settlement. But immediately afterwards, in the Old Forest, we find ourselves in a place whose history reaches back to the very origins of Middle-earth. The incident in the barrow-downs, too, highlights the importance of the (not always peacefully resting) past.

The general impression one gets from Elrond's home is not one of otherworldly 'timelessness', though. After all, houses are rather down-to-earth affairs and elves are normally not brought into too close a connection with dwellings. Lothlórien, in contrast, has roots that go back to a former age and belongs to a category of places that, with the beginning of the Fourth Age, have begun to disappear for good from Middle-earth. If compared with each other, Elrond's home in Rivendell could be characterised as being an 'archive of stories and tales' with the Hall of Fire as the 'reading room'. Lothlórien, then, where elvish history is not yet dead, represents the 'living past'.

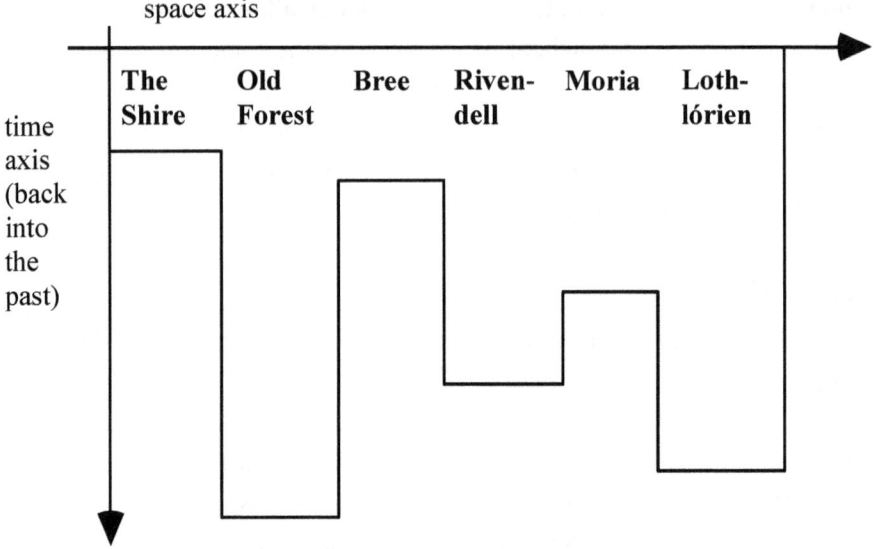

After leaving Lothlórien, the narrative unity of the plot finds an end and parallel strands of action force us to switch regularly from one point of view to another. This means, on the level of space, that the so far sequential and monolinear presentation of places ends. The former unity of space and time is superseded by a multiple view which simultaneously opens up new horizons that are developed parallel to the divergent subplots. This means an almost exponential increase in spatial development and the reader is 'flooded' with new vistas. Yet, since the basics have been established within the first part of the book, it is not necessary to analyse the ensuing development in order to understand Tolkien's use of space and place. The gain in knowledge would be merely one of quantity, and not of quality.

5 HABITATIO EST OMEN

It is crucial for our argument that Tolkien introduces his peoples in their natural habitats. The exception to this rule are dwarves and orcs. Since dwarves are a secretive, heavily industrialised people (mining and ironworking), their settlements were probably not as attractive to depict as those of other races. The 'problem of the habitat of the orcs' will be treated later on.

A hobbit without his hole and the Shire is no real hobbit. The hobbit-hole, on a small scale, and the Shire on a larger one, are the spatial equivalents to their inhabitants. Habitat and dweller have been fused into a harmonious and symbiotic union. A similar positive correspondance can only be found in Lothlórien. There, the forest seems to have taken on more and more 'elvish' qualities during the milleniums of its existence. Yet the influence has been mutual. The elves of Lothlórien call themselves 'Galadhrim', i.e. 'tree-people' (LotR:359). Sam Gamgee's pertinent comment shows this mutual dependency (LotR:380):

> Now these folk aren't wanderers or homeless, and seem a bit nearer to the likes of us: they seem to belong here, more even than Hobbits do in the Shire. Whether they've made the land, or the land's made them, it's hard to say, if you take my meaning.

These two examples of symbiotic unity are only surpassed once, namely in connection with the characterisation of ents. These tree-herds not only live among trees, but they have sometimes the tendency to develop in direction of trees, to become 'treeish'. Furthermore, the habitat of the ents, the Forest of Fangorn, carries the name of the oldest ent, 'Fangorn', i.e. 'Treebeard' in Common Speech. This way inhabitant and habitat even fall together on the level of names.

Bree, Rivendell, and also Moria are either too open and multicultural or too changed as to provide a similar prototypical characterisation of their inhabitants like the more isolated and screened off homelands of the Shire and Lothlórien. Bree and Elrond's home are places where people from all over Middle-earth come together, and they primarily fulfil a different narrative function than to characterise their inhabitants. This is why these places do not feature prominently but remain in the background and provide the unobtrusive setting for the action. Moria, the former pride of the dwarves, is only the pale reflection of the once splendid and magnificent underground-city built by a powerful and rich people.

So far we have been able to characterise the non-human races (hobbits, elves, ents, and, to some extent, dwarves) by means of their typical habitats (the Shire, Lothlórien, Fangorn, Moria). For the human race, however, this is no longer possible. Men in Middle-earth are very much a race on the move and are to be found in the most diverse habitats. Even though we see quite a bit of Middle-earth, there are only two human nations that we get to know better. These are first the Rohirrim, the Riders of the Mark, and second the Gondoreans around whose capital Minas Tirith the battle rages. In contrast to the other mortal yet nonhuman races, the description of places and homesteads plays a minor role in the characterisation of men. Words and deeds are of much greater importance.[7] This contrast comes beautifully to the fore in Treebeard's gnomic verses (LotR:485):

> Learn now the lore of Living Creatures!
> First name the four, the free peoples:
> Eldest of all, the elf-children;
> Dwarf the delver, dark are his houses;
> Ent the earthborn, old as mountains;
> Man the mortal, master of horses:

Pippin adds a line for the hobbits (LotR:486):

> Half-grown hobbits, the hole-dwellers.

In these lines, dwarves as well as hobbits get explicitly characterised by means of their respective dwelling-places, which seem, for the ents, to

---

[7] The Rohirrim, at least, seem to develop something like a symbiotic unity with their habitat, which finds reflection in the character of their language. See Legolas' comment on their language (LotR:530): "'That, I guess, is the language of the Rohirrim,' said Legolas; 'for it is like to this land itself; rich and rolling in part, and else hard and stern as the mountains.'"

contain the quintessence of these two races.[8] The third mortal people, men, are defined by the adjective 'mortal' and their activity as horse-breeders – which indirectly points to their relative lack of rootedness. Although it is not possible to characterise the entire human race by means of their habitat, we do find communities that are defined by a more or less typical habitat, e.g. the Wasa of the Drúadan forest, or nations whose area of settlement has a centre of identity, as e.g. Minas Tirith for Gondor.[9]

6 THE PROBLEM OF THE ORCS

The orcs, in contrast to the even least stationary of the free peoples (mankind), do not enter into a creative interaction with their environment. We never encounter them in their original homeland, if there is such a thing at all – which is to be doubted. Orcs are 'secondary creations' by Melkor, i.e. perverse apings of their fairer counterparts, the elves. They are not original creatures and thus lack an original homeland. Tolkien may mention cities, settlements and strongholds populated by orcs, but he never describes them in any detail. We encounter the orcs as conquerors and occupants of the deserted dwarf-city of Moria, in military camps around Isengard or Mordor, or in the originally man-built citadels of Cirith Ungol and Minas Morgul, but never in any genuine orc-habitat. We know little about their geographic distribution, and we know even less about their social structure. The orcs are even more 'desocialised' than the elves and dwarves (from a narratological point of view) and we find them in no other form than the military unit of varying size. The orcs are to be found on the one end of the scale of socialisation. At the opposite end we find hobbits and men, who are reported to marry, to have children, relatives, acquaintances and friends.

---

8   In the ring-poem, both dwarves and elves are characterised by means of their habitat (LotR:64): "Three Rings for the Elven-kings under the sky, / Seven for the Dwarf-lords in their halls of stone".

9   The name 'Drúadan' most likely derives from the Sindarin word 'Drúedain' which contains 'drû' = 'wose' and 'edain' = 'man'. The name of the forest ('Wose-man Forest') therefore reflects the affinity between place and inhabitants.

The amount of explicitly mentioned socialisation decreases with dwarves and elves who take up a middle position. Their family life is hardly ever mentioned and one has to delve into the appendices to unearth some information about dwarf-women and elf family relationships. For orcs, however, not even the appendices yield any such information. The militarily organised tribe, which excludes women, children and old people, seems to be the basic social unit. It would be unimaginable that Tolkien depicted a tired orc-warrior returning home to his family from a hard day's work of pillage and slaughter. Orcs are, therefore, Tolkien's people without homeland, restless, invading the dwelling-places of other peoples and breeding like maggots.

Furthermore, it is typical for them that they are unable to interact positively with their surroundings. All they can achieve is the destruction and perversion of places they take over. Even Mordor, the seat of evil, has not always been the chaotic, lifeless, perverted and waste landscape it is now – as the few remnants of vegetation and water remind us. And it may not remain a ruined desert forever. Even here, right in the heart of darkness, the reader is reminded that evil has no proper place of its own, that it may pervert a place, yet that it cannot create space.[10] On the one hand, this means that, due to the 'Melkor ingredient' (Chr. Tolkien 1994:400), all places outside the Blessed Realm can be perverted – as happens to some extent even to the Shire. On the other hand, created space is basically positive and, given time and opportunity, even the worst wounds may be healed – as the cases of the Shire and Ithilien prove.

Therefore, to put it in a nutshell, to inhabit a place and to interact positively with it is a typical characteristic of good people. Evil ones, in contrast, have no roots and destroy and pervert the places they occupy.

---

10 The destructive-perverting power of Melkor is most clearly presented in *The Silmarillion* (»Ainulindale – the Music of the Ainur«, pp. 23-24). Tolkien shares in this point St. Augustine's view that evil is the absence of good, i.e. that evil is a negative force in every sense of the meaning.

7 SUMMARY AND CONCLUSION

The places of Middle-earth acquire their symbolic meaning by means of three often related processes.

First, the process of creating a fictional literary universe within the narrative relies on the spatio-geographical as well as historio-temporal development of the various places. In addition to this, the relative position of a passage within the narrative often further determines its function. Thus, the fact that the detailed description of the Shire is placed right at the beginning of *The Lord of the Rings* is to a great extent responsible for its 'archetypicity'. All other places that follow are implicitly compared with the Shire.

Second, the description of the habitat of a people is an important instrument to characterise its inhabitants and supplements or even replaces a straightforward characterisation. Tolkien strongly favours the primacy of the spatial dimension – a predilection obvious in his drawings –, although people may also impress their mark upon a place. Hobbits are the prime example for this. For generations, the hobbits of the Shire have lived a sheltered and quiet life in their country, cultivated the landscape with great love and dedication. Thus, over the centuries, they have become synonymous with their homeland so that a hobbit out of the Shire is like a fish out of the water.

And last, the assignment of a homeland to a people implies a tacit approval. In a sense, the lack of a place of origin, of a home, points to a moral deficiency. Orcs, as the most common representatives of evil, are presented as homeless and destructive invaders and are thus placed in opposition to the hobbits who live in symbiotic harmony with their environment.

Space and time have not allowed us to discuss exhaustively Tolkien's achievement in his creation of Middle-earth. All the same, I hope that the analysis of the basic processes of Tolkien's 'art of sub-creation' has given some insight into the construction of his literary universe. I would like to conclude by alluding to Tolkien's own words about his work – "the book is too short" (LotR:10) –: the paper is, compared to the dimensions of its subject, far too short.

REFERENCES

CARPENTER, Humphrey (Editor, with the assistance of Christopher TOLKIEN). 1981. *Letters of J.R.R. Tolkien*. London: George Allen & Unwin.

– – –. 1977. *J.R.R. Tolkien – A Biography*. London: George Allen & Unwin.

DAY, David. 1991. *Tolkien: The Illustrated Encyclopaedia*. Reprinted as paperback 1993. London: Mitchell Beazley.

– – –. 1994. *Tolkien's Ring*. London: HarperCollins.

DOWIE, William. 1979. »The Gospel of Middle-Earth according to J.R.R. Tolkien.« In: Mary Salu and Robert T. Farrell (eds.). 1979. *J.R.R. Tolkien, Scholar and Storyteller*. Essays in Memoriam. Ithaca and London: Cornell University Press, 265-285.

DURIEZ, Colin. 1992. *The J.R.R. Tolkien Handbook*. Grand Rapids, Michigan: Baker Book House.

FONSTAD, Karen Wynn. 1992. *The Atlas of Middle-Earth*. 2nd revised edition. First edition 1981. Reprinted as paperback 1994. London: HarperCollins.

GIDDINGS, Robert und Elizabeth HOLLAND. 1981. *J.R.R. Tolkien: The Shores of Middle-earth*. London: Junction Books.

HELMS, Randel. 1974. *Tolkien's World*. London: Thames and Hudson.

HETMANN, Frederik. 1984. *Die Freuden der Fantasy: Von Tolkien bis Ende*. Wien: Ullstein.

NOEL, Ruth S. 1977. *The Mythology of Middle-Earth*. Boston: Houghton Mifflin.

– – –. 1980. *The Languages of Tolkien's Middle-earth*. First published 1974. Boston: Houghton Mifflin.

PESCH, Helmut W. (ed.). 1984. *J.R.R. Tolkien – der Mythenschöpfer*. Edition Futurum 5. Meitingen: Corian.

PETZOLD, Dieter. 1980. *J.R.R. Tolkien: 'Fantasy Literature' als Wunscherfüllung und Weltdeutung*. Heidelberg: Carl Winter Universitätsverlag.

ROSEBURY, Brian. 1992. *Tolkien: A Critical Assessment*. New York: St. Martin's Press.

SHIPPEY, Tom A. 1992. *The Road to Middle Earth*. 2nd revised edition. First edition 1982. London: Grafton.

SIBLEY, Brian (text) and John HOWE (illustrations). 1994. *The Map of Tolkien's Middle-earth*. London: HarperCollins.

STEVENS, David and Carol D. STEVENS. 1993. *J.R.R. Tolkien: The Art of the Myth-Maker*. Revised edition. First edition 1992. San Bernardino, California: The Borgo Press.

STRACHEY, Barbara. 1992. *Journeys of Frodo: An Atlas of J.R.R. Tolkien's 'The Lord of the Rings'*. Reprint of the first edition of 1981. London: Grafton.

TOLKIEN, Christopher (ed.). 1979. *Pictures by J.R.R. Tolkien*. Boston: Houghton Mifflin.

――― (ed.). 1985. *J.R.R. Tolkien: The Book of Lost Tales, Part I*. The History of Middle-Earth Volume 1. Original edition 1983. London: HarperCollins.

――― (ed.). 1994. *J.R.R. Tolkien: Morgoth's Ring*. The History of Middle-Earth Volume 10. Original edition 1993. London: HarperCollins.

TOLKIEN, J.R.R. 1938/39. »On Fairy-Stories.« Reprinted 1988 in *Tree and Leaf*. London: Grafton.

―――. 1968. *The Lord of the Rings*. One-volume edition. Text of the 2nd revised edition of 1966. First edition 1954-1956 in 3 volumes. Reprinted as paperback 1992. London: Grafton.

―――. 1977. *The Silmarillion*. Edited by Christopher Tolkien. Reprinted as paperback 1994. London: HarperCollins.

―――. 1981. *The Hobbit*. 4th edition. Original edition 1937. London: Unwin Paperbacks.

TYLER, J.E.A. 1975. *The Tolkien Companion*. London: Macmillan.

Middle-earth: The Collectible Card Game

Powerplay in the World of Tolkien

PATRICK NÄF

Summary

What are collectible card games and what do they have to do with the work of J.R.R. Tolkien? This essay is an attempt to answer these questions – notably by looking at the newest product of the game company *Iron Crown Enterprises* (ICE). MECCG – in full *Middle-earth: The Collectible Card Game* – is but a fresh example of the 'excesses' eager Tolkien fandom can generate. However, as this essay contains few critical elements I am not going to discuss whether this specific 'excess' is a negative or a positive one. I neither want to write a review nor deal with – admittedly interesting – topics such as whether the *Collectible Card Game* will outlive its commercial roots.[1] Rather, I would like to tempt the interested reader with a short introduction to MECCG.

1 ABOUT COLLECTIBLE CARD GAMES

History

MECCG is, as the acronym implies, a so-called *Collectible Card Game*. It is based on J.R.R. Tolkien's imaginary world Middle-earth. Yet, what should one make of the term *Collectible Card Game*? The closest one can probably get are those baseball and football pictures that most children collect avidly at one time or another.

Now, once upon a time there was a very clever games designer called Richard Garfield who asked himself why one should not, in addition to collecting them, also be able to play with these cards. In the summer of

---

[1] On 21 September 1999, Iron Crown Enterprises announced that they would cease the production and sale of all their Middle-earth products. This was no big surprise and just a logical follow-up to their file for bankruptcy on 27 August 1999 and the ensuing license withdrawal by Tolkien Enterprises. Effectively, this meant the commercial death of MECCG, although today you can still find references to fandom activities all over the internet.

1993 the result of this inspired question was released upon the world when the American company *Wizards of the Coast* (WotC) introduced *Magic: the Gathering*. *Magic*, as people prefer to call it, was the first and to date most successful representative of its kind. Today it still prevails on the market as the best-known *Collectible Card Game* and is distributed more widely than any other game in its class on earth.

In 1993 nobody had any idea what a gigantic success *Magic* would become during the following months and years. Rather, the people of WotC were concerned with the question whether it would be possible to strip the game of its freak-status at all. This assessment soon had to be revised; within the shortest time imaginable the first editions of *Magic* were sold out and the market yelled for more! WotC, and in their wake their competitors, began to recognise the potential marketability of this newly discovered product and hurriedly endeavoured to fill the forming vacuum. TSR was one of the first companies to produce an imitation of *Magic*, which was named *Spellfire*. It is based on another popular favourite, the well-known AD&D. Soon dozens of games flooded the market but most of them were not very successful. They either failed because of the overwhelming dominance of *Magic* or because of their own inherent shortcomings. As was to be expected, most of the newcomers were cheap imitations lacking a concept as well as a clear-cut design. Not surprisingly they disappeared as fast as they were produced – *Spellfire* included.

Apart from *Magic* those *Collectible Card Games* that have succeeded are, as a rule, those that have been able to fall back on a famous name. Examples for this are *Star Trek*, *Star Wars* but also MECCG. Nevertheless, a few altogether new games have also been able to hold their own on the market, for instance *Guardians, Legend of the Five Rings* or *Netrunner* (if I have been amiss by not mentioning someone's favourite game I herewith beseech his or her forgiveness). Today the market has calmed down; fewer new publications are issued while the prevailing games' output of cards is still extremely high. Only *DragonDice*, a *Collectible Dice Game* produced by TSR, can to some extent be termed original.

Fundamental Principles

Magic, as the first game of its kind, is the best example for the classic principles that are typical of a *Collectible Card Game*:

- The games are, of course, based on cards (thus *Collectible **Card** Game*).
- Each card belongs to a limited edition. That confers a certain value upon each card in the eyes of collectors (thus ***Collectible** Card Game*). The basic set is printed in large quantities and the composition of its cards is changed every now and then. The basic set contains many cards with fundamental functions and therefore provides an easy introduction to the game. As an addition to the basic set new editions, the so-called expansion sets, are issued periodically. Expansion sets are designed around special topics and usually appear in a much more limited edition than the basic set does.
- Each card has its own rarity value; some cards simply are issued in bigger quantities than others.
- The point is, of course, that all these various cards can be used for playing (thus *Collectible Card **Game***).
- Depending on the edition, cards are sold in packs of different sizes whose contents vary randomly. As a norm there are but two different sizes: the big starter pack and the smaller booster pack. In principle a starter pack enables anyone to play a full game – at least after studying the rules. Booster packs, however, provide the possibility to buy smaller amounts of cards at one time.
- In addition to the information needed to play the game, each card is adorned with a picture. Each picture is designed by an artist exclusively for this specific card which gives each card a special touch and makes for an aesthetically pleasing game. If an artist's pictures are popular they can influence the value of a card.
- Thanks to the chance packaging there often is lively trading between players, respectively collectors. If someone feels an urgent desire to play with a specific card or if someone is looking for a card missing from his

or her collection it is usually cheaper to barter for it instead of buying several boosters hoping that one of them will contain the coveted card. The trading aspect is responsible for the *Collectible Card Games'* second name *Trading Card Games* (TCG).
- Generally speaking, there are two formats for playing. On the one hand, there are fun matches among friends. On the other, there are serious matches during official tournaments where money or prestige are of importance. In this regard *Magic* again plays a leading role. In 1997 *Magic* world-championships took place for the third time. And, of course, they had to be preceded by a series of local qualification tournaments and national championships.

2 MIDDLE EARTH: THE COLLECTIBLE CARD GAME

Let us now take a closer look at MECCG. Bearing in mind the general characteristics of *Collectible Card Games* mentioned in the previous chapter, I now want to make some observations on how MECCG differs from the norm and where it is typical for its kind.

MECCG is very **typical** in regard to the quantity of cards produced. Since it was first issued Christmas 1995 no less than five sets have been published.

- *Middle-earth: The Wizards* (METW) is the basic set and contains about 480 cards. It initially appeared at the end of 1995, first in a limited (cards with a black border), then in an unlimited edition (cards with a blue border). Now, $1^1/_2$ years later, the unlimited edition remains unchanged.
- *Middle-earth: The Dragons* is the first expansion set and contains about 180 cards.
- *Middle-earth: Dark Minions* is the second expansion set and also contains about 180 cards.
- *Middle-earth: The Lidless Eye* is an independent, stand-alone set and is intended to be a counterpart to the basic set METW. Accordingly, this

edition contains about 420 card. *Lidless Eye* cards (and the expansion sets going with it) cannot be used in the same set as METW cards, thus the term stand-alone. However, instead of individual cards one can combine the two decks – for instance by playing a *Lidless Eye* deck against a METW deck.

- *Middle-earth: Against the Shadow* is the first expansion set specifically developed for *Lidless Eye*. It contains about 150 cards.[2]

Up to today more than 1400 different cards have been designed for MECCG alone. Furthermore, there are six promotional cards not included in any set. As designated collectors' items, they were only placed in certain newsmagazines and other published media to attract publicity. The magnitude of this scale proves that MECCG is one of the most successful games on the market right now. (In comparison: *Magic* contains about 2200 cards at the moment.)

By the way, as customary for *Collectible Card Games,* all cards have differing rarity values.

As is **typical** of *Collectible Card Games*, MECCG is sold in starter and booster packs. **Atypical** is, on the other hand, that starter packs do not contain a chance selection of cards. If MECCG cards were selected randomly it would seriously impair the starter pack's potential to be played on its own. Only a sensibly balanced combination is able to ensure a highly enjoyable first game. Unlike other *Collectible Card Games* MECCG starter packs contain cards which are co-ordinated, which in turn upgrades its worth as a game. While other games give the impression of chaotic

---

2   Until its commercial death in 1999, 2 more sets were published:
- *Middle-earth: The White Hand* is an expansion set compatible to both the basic set METW and the *Lidless Eye*. It contains 122 cards.
- *Middle-earth: The Balrog* is the last ever produced MECCG expansion set. It appeared in December 1998, consists of 104 cards and is playable together with other cards from earlier expansion sets.

disorganisation, *Middle-earth* motivates the beginner to further investigate the intricate depths of the game.

In regard to the artwork MECCG clearly surpasses its competitors. It is **atypical** in that it is well designed. More about this in the last passage of this paper.

With respect to trading one can say that collectors have not gone to the same excess as with *Magic*. However, MECCG does possess all necessary qualifications for a *Trading Card Game*.

I have not heard about official tournaments taking place in Switzerland. Nevertheless, ICE tries to provide a certain quality control world-wide through the so called *Council of Endor*.

We have now defined the specific characteristics of MECCG as a *Collectible Card Game*. The next question will be: What have the producers thought of in order to fit the game into the world of Tolkien?

3 MIDDLE EARTH: THE BACKGROUND

MECCG is a game that can be played by more than two people. The basic idea is that each player embodies one of the five wizards (Gandalf, Saruman, Radagast, Alatar or Pallando).[3] The five wizards' aim is to find support in their battle against Sauron – first in secrecy, later quite openly. The fact that the players/wizards are competing with each other (everybody wants to win the game, right?) instead of working together like they do in Tolkien's work (at least that was the idea) is explained away by twisting the story slightly. In MECCG the story goes that each wizard has his own ideas about how Sauron should be defeated and attempts to enforce his ideas on the Free Council.

The Free Council is an assembly of the leaders of the Free Peoples. It is called together at the end of a game and during its course each

---

3   Expansion sets later added more aspects to the basic game, such as a player taking on the role of a Ringwraith (*Lidless Eye*), a fallen wizard (*The White Hand*) or a Balrog (*The Balrog*)

wizard/player is judged according to the amount of prestige and support he has been able to gather during the game. In the future the Free Peoples will follow the advice of the wizard who comes off best: he thus wins the game.

To gain reputation and seek assistance, the wizard has to travel from site to site to win factions and allies for his cause or to find objects that could further his purpose. On his quests, the wizard has to overcome numerous obstacles for which Sauron and his servants are responsible. To master such difficulties the wizard has to gather friends who, at the beginning of the game, travel for him – and later with him – through the lands.

Travelling rates high in MECCG. In this respect the game keeps closely to its source, Tolkien's *Lord of the Rings*, in which the Quest, i.e. the attempt to destroy the One Ring, is a major theme. A player can only win if he or she sends his or her wizard and his companions on various journeys. The wizard has to be able to visit places where he can earn the reputation necessary for winning. Besides, the influence of Sauron and his servants cannot take effect until the parties are on their way. Those that stick to a safe place might not have to fear any evil but at the same time they will have no chance in hell to carry the game.

The above is a description of the setting and aims of MECCG in general terms. Though the precise concept of the game will be introduced in the next two chapters I will here take the opportunity to quickly explain how the reputation of each wizard is quantified during the convention of the Free Council. It is a point system: whenever a wizard wins a new ally or secures the support of a whole faction, whenever he finds powerful objects or discharges tasks assigned to him, he will receive a number of so called **marshalling points**, which will be credited to his account. As soon as the wizard/player has managed to collect twenty points or more he or she has the right to bring the game to its conclusion (though the other players each have an additional turn in which to gain the missing points to draw or even to take the lead). The next step is to call the Free Council together and to add up points. Whoever accounts for the most marshalling points wins. (Analogous to the *Lord of the Rings* one can also triumph by employing the time-honoured method of destroying the One Ring at Mount Doom or by eliminating one's competitors, respectively one's fellow wizards.)

In principle we now know how to win a game but presumably no-one has as yet understood how the game *really* proceeds. Therefore I would like to concentrate on the actual game itself by introducing first the tangible game components, namely the cards, and then the rules how to use these cards.

4 MIDDLE EARTH: THE CARDS

In this and the next chapter we will deal exclusively with the basic set *Middle-earth: The Wizards*, short METW. Although new cards and rules were introduced with the publication of the first expansion set, *The Dragons*, I will limit myself to the original game which in itself has much to give. Those of you who would like to know more should buy one of the booster packs as each contains a little pamphlet explaining the extra rules.

Now to the cards. METW is divided into five categories of cards. Each category has a different function. Most of the cards are based on motifs from the books of Tolkien, be it people, a place or an event. A few, however, are not 'real', they are 'invented' (so much to the perception of reality by ardent Tolkienists). These are made up by the games designers and only distantly related to Tolkien's Middle-earth.

The five categories are:

- Characters
- Regions
- Sites
- Hazards
- Resources

Characters

In order to be easily recognised these cards have a blue background. Each card depicts a more or less important or well-known personality from Tolkien's story. The concept behind the game (see next chapter) requires that only 'good' characters find their way into this category, so for instance Galadriel, Aragorn or Frodo. Five special character cards represent the five Istari: Saruman, Gandalf, Radagast, Pallando, and Alatar.

Regions

These cards differ substantially from the other cards. They not only look different but also they are not used if the game is played according to beginners' rules. Region cards represent large geographical areas through which the characters have to travel to reach their goal, i.e. the next site (see next category). The entire map of Middle-earth as we know it from the *Lord of the Rings* is divided into 52 regions. Examples are Rohan, Forochel or Gorgoroth.

Sites

These cards have a white background. The places represented by site cards have – in contrast to region cards – geographically narrow boundaries. Here characters are able to instigate certain events during the game. Let me express it in this manner: regions are the way, sites destinations. As sites we get Dol Guldur, Minas Tirith or also Weathertop. In addition there are four special site cards, the so-called Havens which I will discuss later on. The four Havens are Rivendell, Lórien, the Grey Havens, and Edhellond.

Hazards

In accord with their general motif hazard cards have a black background. These cards can only be played when it is **not** the player's turn. They represent the dangers and obstacles with which Sauron and his servants try to terrorise characters on their way. Examples extend from simple bad luck, to attacks by wargs or ambushing orcs, and encounters with the seriously bad guys, the Nazgûls.

Resources

These cards sport a brown background. There are four subcategories of resources: items (for instance Glamdring, the One Ring), factions (for instance the Men of Dorwinion, the Iron Hill Dwarves), allies (Tom Bombadil, Shadowfax) and events (Favor of the Valar, Praise of Elbereth). Resource cards are principally positive cards; they help a wizard to reach his goal of collecting 20 marshalling points. A few contribute marshalling points, others mitigate the results of hazard cards, and so on.

Next follows an in-depth examination of the rules in an attempt to elucidate the use of the various cards which I have just introduced.

5 MIDDLE-EARTH: THE RULES

On first sight the rules of METW appear rather complicated and awkward. This impression is enforced by the somewhat sluggish progress of the game, yet in the end it is all a matter of practice. Those that play regularly usually know the rules quite well. And in contrast to the excessive rules that *Magic* produced, METW has rules which are comparatively simple.

Each player starts the game off by positioning up to five characters and two minor items. This rule guarantees that each player can start in whatever way he or she deems fit. At the same time he or she does not have to rely on luck to the extent that other games require. Afterwards the game proceeds in rounds: during every round each player is able to play twice; once to effect his or her own turn and once to place hazard cards during his or her opponent's turn. If more than two players are taking part each player interacts with exactly two of his or her competitors: the one to the left (whom he or she is allowed to attack) and the one to the right (who is able to attack him or her in turn). That way a free-for-all and the ensuing chaos is avoided.

A turn is separated into a series of phases that have to be dealt with sequentially:

- Untap Phase
- Organisation Phase
- Long-event Phase
- Movement/Hazard Phase
- Site Phase
- End-of-turn Phase

As there is no point in painstakingly going through each phase (if I did that the gentle reader could just as well chuck this article and ask me to present him or her with a booklet on the rules) I prefer to present the course of the game in a more pleasing form.

First though I have to admit that I will not always follow the rules in *all* details. The reason for this is simple: my aim is to show how METW is played without downright copying the booklet containing the rules. Of course, I had to compromise somewhat but those familiar with the rules will hopefully forgive me for that. (Though I should not worry overtly much, whosoever knows the game will hardly read this article...will he?)

Let us now grow an additional pair of eyes. That way we are well prepared to peek over professor Tolkien's shoulders as he writes the *Lord of the Rings* while at the same time observing the games designers of ICE.

Sample Turn 1

Our discussion sets in with the eighth chapter of the second book, 'Farewell to Lórien'. The Company is getting ready to continue its journey. Their sojourn in Lórien has allowed them to recover from the trials in the Mines of Moria.	Speaking in terms of the game, the company has just started with its next turn and is now presently in the Untap Phase. Having visited Moria during the last turn, the companions are all very exhausted from their adventures. This exhaustion has been made visible by **tapping** the character-cards, i.e. they are turned by 90°. All tapped characters are untapped during the Untap Phase, i.e. they return back to normal and are ready for action again.
Thanks to the healing power of the elves, even Frodo's spear-wound, which has been inflicted on him by the ork-chieftain in the Chamber of Mazarbul, has been healed.	Not only characters that are tapped, but also those that are wounded (turned by 180°) can be healed at Lórien. This is because Lórien is a **Haven**. The wounded characters remain tapped though, which is meant to indicate that they are still worn out.
Since Gandalf had been, as usual, rather taciturn concerning his plans, the Company does not know for certain which way to take. Yet, they know that, for the time being, they have to follow the course of the Anduin. The three elven-boats, a gift from Celeborn, will help them to postpone the decision. It is only when they have to leave the boats behind that they must make up their minds – which will be at the feet of Amon Hen, above the Rauros falls.	After the Untap Phase comes the **Organisation Phase**. It is now that the route for the following Movement/Hazard Phase is decided on. The player selects a **site card** which stands for the next destination of his or her company. He or she also chooses the region cards that connect the point of departure with their destination. As mentioned above, the regions can be seen as the way, and the sites as the destinations. Amon Hen is the destination in our example and the way leads the company through the regions 'Wold & Foothills' (where the site of departure, Lórien, is situated) and 'Rohan' (where Amon Hen is to be found).
Thus, Frodo and his companions say goodbye to Lothlórien with a heavy heart and continue their journey south.	'A turn' implies passing of time; thus, no more than four regions may be crossed, namely the region of the site of departure, the region of the site of destination and two additional regions in between the two.
It will take them some days to reach Amon Hen, and during this time some strange and disturbing events occur.	The Movement Phase proper follows after the Organisation Phase, during which the journey has been planned (we omit the intermediary Long-event Phase for the time being). While the company is 'on the road', it is constantly threatened by various dangers. This is why the entire phase is called **Movement/Hazard Phase**.

Middle-earth: The Collectable Card Game – Powerplay in the World of Tolkien

Gollum puts in an appearance or two and, after the close escape at the cataracts of Sarn Gebir, a group of orcs attacks the Company. Yet even something more sinister and threatening hovers high above their heads and it is only Legolas' enchanted arrow that is able to ward off the danger.	It is only during this phase that our adversary is able to interfere actively to our disadvantage. In order to do so, he or she plays different **hazard cards** which hinder, wound or even kill our characters. The dangerousness of the hazards depends on the region or site-type. Coastal Seas and Free-domains are comparatively safe areas, whereas Shadow-lands and Dark-domains are highly dangerous. Since orcs are a widespread nuisance all over Eriador, and since they are not Sauron's top cracks, the opponent may play the hazard card *Orc Patrol* at almost any time and place. Nazgûl hazard cards, on the contrary, are to be used in a very limited way – such as in the Dark-domains, since there the characters find themselves in areas which are under Sauron's direct control.
The Company has, at last, reached the meadow of Parth Galen at the feet of Amon Hen. There they rest for the night and postpone the decision on the direction to take till the next morning.	The next phase, after the Movement/Hazard Phase, is the **Site Phase**. The characters have arrived at their destination, i.e. Amon Hen. Each site offers a variety of things to do. However, the character who wants to profit from these opportunities and do something, must be rested, i.e. be untapped. Frodo, who has to make the final decision, is yet not fully recovered from the orc-attack which took place during the Movement/Hazard Phase, i.e. he is still tapped. Therefore, the decision has to be postponed for one turn. This allows Frodo to recover, i.e. become untapped. Thus, nothing happens during the Site Phase and we conclude the turn with the End-of-Turn Phase.

Sample Turn 2

Aragorn presents the various possible choices on the next morning. Since Frodo has to carry the burden of the Ring, it is he who has to decide on the future of the Fellowship.	We start with an Untap Phase. All characters, including Frodo, are untapped. Nothing happens during the Organisation Phase; nor does anything occur during the Long-event Phase and the Movement/Hazard Phase.
Frodo asks for one hour time for reflection and, since he wishes to be alone, he wanders off along the feet of Amon Hen. Driven to the top of Amon Hen by the incident with Boromir, Frodo becomes aware of Mordor's preparations for war and decides to carry the Ring on his own into Mordor and	As mentioned above, there is the possibility to do something during the Site Phase. The site Amon Hen, for example, offers the opportunity to gather **information** from its high seat – which Frodo does. In other sites, characters may look for more or less powerful items (such as the dwarf-rings in Moria or the Arkenstone at the Lonely Mountain), they may gain the support of **allies** (such as Treebeard in Wellinghall) or of entire peoples (such as the Rohirrim in Edoras) and other powerful **factions**. Information, items, allies and factions are resource-cards and, if successfully played during the Site Phase, they provide the **Marshalling Points** which

destroy it in the Cracks of Doom.	are necessary for victory. Frodo thus tries to gather information on Amon Hen which may help him to reach a decision, but ...
Before he is able to put his resolution into practice, he must escape discovery by the searching Red Eye of Mordor. And his friends, too, have to weather an orc attack during which Boromir gets killed.	... apart from the dangers brought about by the opponent while the company is travelling across the regions of Middle-earth (in the Movement/Hazard Phase), there are many sites that host unpleasant surprises. The characters remain untroubled as long as they do not attempt to do something at such a site (e.g. to play a resource card, which would provide Marshalling Points). Yet, as soon as they start to look for items or, as in our example on Amon Hen, try to collect information, the hostile forces of the site are awakened. Since these forces are 'site-inherent' and not controlled by the opponent, they are simply called **automatic attacks**. They range from staple orc-attacks to more challenging dragon-raids on the Withered Heath or to troll-attacks in Barad-dûr.

Sample Turn 3

The Fellowship of the Ring splits up immediately after the incidents at Amon Hen: • Frodo and Sam try to find a way in the direction of the Dead Marshes • Merry and Pippin are first abducted by the orcs and then stay in Fangorn • Aragorn, Legolas and Gimli first search for Merry and Pippin and later on depart together with Gandalf from Fangorn to Edoras	So far the characters have been united in one single company which was moving from site to site. Yet it is equally possible to assign the characters to various groups during the Organisation Phase and to send them off in different directions. We have now entered the Organisation Phase and the three groups (cf. column on the left) reside in the following points of departure: • Frodo and Sam: Amon Hen • Merry and Pippin: Wellinghall • Aragorn, Legolas and Gimli: Wellinghall The route taken by each group is given by the region and destination-site cards put down: • Frodo and Sam: regions: Brown Lands, Dagorlad; destination: Dead Marshes • Merry and Pippin: regions: Fangorn, Gap of Isen; destination: Isengard • Aragorn, Legolas and Gimli: regions: Fangorn, Rohan; destination: Edoras

Aragorn, Legolas and Gimli meet a strange old man in Fangorn. He turns out to be Gandalf who was believed dead and who is now no longer Gandalf the Grey, but Gandalf the White!	During the Organisation Phase, the routes of the various groups are planned, groups may be united, but also new character-cards may be brought into play. In our case, it is Gandalf himself who makes his entry. If a player reveals himself as wizard, he may profit from this action since wizards are very powerful and strong character cards. However, there is a risk involved: if the opponent succeeds in eliminating this one character, then all is lost at once.
	We will again focus on the Site Phase and thus omit the Long-event Phase and the Movement/Hazard Phase and proceed directly to the Site Phase.
After having scaled the cliffs of Emyn Muil, Sam and Frodo see themselves confronted with Gollum, who has been following them for quite a while. They capture him and Frodo makes him swear allegiance by the Ring. This way, Gollum the Enemy becomes, at least for the time being, Sméagol the Ally.	The group consisting of Frodo and Sam has reached the destination of the Dead Marshes. In order to increase their Marshalling Points, they try and play a kind of resource-card, i.e. an **ally** – that is, in this case, Gollum. Allies are characters that are not brought into play during the Organisation Phase, but during the Site Phase. Also, they cannot be directly controlled by means of a wizard/player, but they follow the one character who has sought them out and persuaded them to come along – so to speak.
Aragorn, Legolas and Gimli have joined forces with Gandalf and make haste to get to Meduseld, the Hall of the Kings of Rohan in Edoras. They want to win Theoden's confidence and thus the support of the Rohirrim.	The group headed by Gandalf wants to acquire Marshalling Points, too. They try their luck with another kind of resource-card, a **faction**, in our case the one of the Rohirrim. Since factions have to be persuaded to join a company, one of the characters has to successfully attempt an influence roll so that the Marshalling Points do really count towards the victory.
After Treebeard and also the other Ents have come to trust Merry and Pippin, they march off in direction of Isengard.	Merry and Pippin have been successful at winning over the Ent-faction and thus stock up their Marshalling Points account. They wait at Isengard till Gandalf and his companions, all of whom will come from Helm's Deep, are going to join them.

Sample Turn 4

The part of the Fellowship around Gandalf rides towards Isengard after the victorious battle at Helm's Deep. In Isengard, they come across Merry and Pippin in the ruined gatehouse.	It is not only possible to create several travelling companies, but it is also possible to unite some of those who happen to be at the same site during the Organisation Phase and thus to form a larger and more powerful group.

In our case, the group of Merry and Pippin unites with the one of Gandalf, Aragorn, Gimli, Legolas and Theoden at the site of Isengard (Gandalf & Co. have arrived during the preceding turn). |
| The reunited companions are overjoyed that they have found each other again and for the moment it looks as if the danger west of the Anduin has been averted. The sun shines brightly and they settle down to a pleasant meal, enjoy a smoke of pipeweed and even start to tell stories. | Now, at long last, comes the **Long-event Phase**. During this phase, the player may bring cards into the game whose effects last longer than one turn, yet which is nevertheless limited. There are both hazard as well as resource long-event cards. Long-events last for one round, i.e. till all players have finished their moves. Also, they are not keyed to characters, but affect the whole of Middle-earth.

Our opponent does not play any long-event hazards. We, on the contrary, activate the long-event resource-card 'Sun'. The strength of all Dunedain characters is increased during one turn. We want to protect our company against possible attacks during the ensuing Movement/Hazard Phase. Since long-events last a whole round, i.e. until it is our turn again, it may be that also our opponent is able to profit from our 'sunny' card – provided he or she features some Dunedain, too. |
| They all gather at the entrance of Orthanc afterwards to listen to the talk with Saruman. He proves himself stubborn and refuses to come to his senses. His attempts to pull the wool over the Company's eyes, however, fail. Thus, Gandalf expells him from the Order and excludes him from the Council of the Wise. Immediately after this, Grima Wormtongue throws the Palantir of Orthanc at Gandalf. The ensuing development shows the usefulness and danger inherent in this item. | The company does not travel but prepares for the talk with Saruman. Therefore nothing happens during the Movement/Hazard Phase. During the Site Phase, Gandalf is able to acquire a palantir, thus gaining both Marshalling and Corruption Points (cf. below).

Saruman, who appears as a negative figure in LotR, is a positive character in METW. In the context of our sample turn, a possible interpretation for this is that the opponent has revealed him or herself as Saruman, and then fails since the character-card of Saruman has been corrupted. |

Following these four sample turns there are a few additional points I would like to mention, particularly:

- The game's concept of 'corruption' is one of the inventors' finest ideas. To explain it quickly, the idea is that characters are affected by different temptations that can cause them to turn away from the Free Peoples. In the *Lord of the Rings* Saruman was corrupted by power. Radagast was less and less interested in his original task and in the end Nature herself corrupted him. Denethor, too, fell from grace through the despair that Sauron had taught him.

    Corruption is represented by certain hazard cards, namely the 'lure' cards. Characters can also be endangered if they gain too much power by collecting potent items (the One Ring is very corruptive, as you might guess). If a character succumbs to corruption he or she is eliminated; if the character is the wizard himself, the game is over for that particular player.

- Some cards have the attribute 'unique'. These cards are special in that only one of the same kind can be used in the same game. If one player uses his or her Shelob, the other one is not allowed to play it even if he or she has it in his or her deck. Characters, allies and factions are, as a rule, 'unique', and the same is true for some of the most powerful items (for instance Durin's Axe, the One Ring) as well as special hazard cards (all Nazgûls, Shelob).

- Marshalling points can also be gained if the characters defeat certain of their rival's hazard cards (so called 'creature' cards) in battle. You can easily imagine that a wizard's prestige raises automatically whenever he and his companions succeed in a fight against Sauron and company. This prevents the game's decline into futile hack 'n' slay. A player has to carefully calculate how strong a creature card he or she can afford to risk against his or her opponent without eliminating his or her own chances at winning the game.

- Playing METW the player always holds eight or more cards in his or her hand. After almost every phase he or she is allowed to replenish his or her hand so as to have eight cards again. During each Movement/Hazard Phase he or she draws at least one if not two or more cards for each of the moving groups of characters. This proves that METW is very lively despite the complex rules. In many matches, one can go almost through the whole stack of cards.

- MECCG is not only a *Collectible Card Game* but also a dice game in some ways. Many decisions are made by a roll of two six-sided dice. Though the game is based on the players' ability to make rational decisions MECCG therefore contains an element of chance. However, no roll of dice can have such a disastrous effect as one might find in other, less balanced games.

I hope that I have managed to explain the possibilities of the game with the help of the four sample turns and the additional remarks in a way that allow you to grasp the basics without having to go out and buy a starter pack.

And now for the last chapter – as always last but not least.

6 MIDDLE EARTH: THE ART

The artistic aspect of MECCG is a very important one, though it does not in itself influence the game. It is nevertheless essential, affecting the whole product. Therefore I want to dedicate a brief chapter of its own to this topic.

Of course, questions of art have always been matters of taste and thus open to discussion – especially if it comes to decide on what rates as 'good' art. I would maintain that MECCG undoubtedly belongs to the elite among *Collectible Card Games*, artistically speaking. In MECCG, in contrast to other *Collectible Card Games*, two fundamentally different and thus usually competing approaches have been combined to make a pleasing whole, namely diversity of artists and unity of style.

Certainly the most striking thing in regard to MECCG's artwork is the fact that all cards have been designed along the same lines. Looking at the cards one immediately recognises that they belong to the same game. However, unlike other *Collectible Card Games*, MECCG is not designed by a single artist to achieve this effect. Neither does it appear as chaotic as some other games that use a lot of artists for variety. MECCG features over forty different artists and nevertheless manages to look... well... finished. This rather admirable feat instantly put MECCG on top of my list of games worth collecting when I first saw it. I collect *Magic* out of a habit and because I am an avid magician, so to say.... To collect MECCG, however, is a pleasure. Not that I have been playing it much or for a long time, but I collect it simply because the game looks good!

Similarly remarkable are the many details that add to the esteem that many Tokien readers have for MECCG. If you know the books and take a closer look at the artwork of the game you will often be able to detect elements from LotR or the *Hobbit*. This proves that at least some of the artists have actually taken the time to read Tolkien's work which creates another link of sympathy to the game.

I think it would be futile to discuss either the existing or missing accuracy of certain single cards at any length in this chapter. I support the point of view that an artist should be allowed to practise his or her own artistic freedom. There is one exception, however, and I would like to point to this bone of contention. If you are familiar with ICE and its MERP products you probably know Angus McBride, doubtlessly one of the best and most successful artists of Tolkien themes. That some of his pictures were incorporated into METW certainly is an enrichment, yet I felt quite disappointed to learn that ICE had simply taken McBride's already existing pictures from MERP instead of letting him furnish the game with new art. In my opinion, this robs METW of some of the originality it could have had, and although this, of course, is not a major issue it should have been considered by the designers of MECCG.

7 CONCLUSION

Only a few words are left to say. If you are quite bemused by my article but still game to try your hand at *Middle-earth*, I would recommend a closer look at the game itself. It would be ideal, of course, if you could peek over somebody's shoulder during an actual game. With continued interest I would suggest the purchase of a starter set and a first try-out – preferably with someone who is able to explain the rules. That way you will get the full benefit of someone else's experience. And do not despair: the rules seem a lot more complicated than they actually are.

Only an interactive game with other people will provide you with the complete gratification – so do not let yourself be discouraged from joining a group of 'gamesters'. Inappropriate scruple concerning age or gender are totally out of place as, in my opinion, people who like to play games are the most genial human beings possible. That, by the way, is universally applicable and not limited to MECCG!

Remember: All work and no play... and along these lines – Merry Gaming!

Middle-earth: the Wizards - the Representation of Tolkien's World in the Game

PETER BUCHS

Summary

J.R.R. Tolkien's imaginary world, Middle-earth, found such a huge and eager following, that his books alone could not quench the thirst for more. As a result, a wide variety of films, radio adaptations and games were made to satisfy this demand. The quality of these representations have to be judged by two criteria. The first one is concerned with their quality as examples of their *genus*, the second one with their quality as representations of Tolkien's world. This paper sets out to describe the various features of the collectable card game *Middle-earth: the Wizards*, notably its cards and some of its rules, and to look at them from the point of view of the latter.

I A FEW REMARKS ABOUT THE REPRESENTATION OF FICTIONAL WORLDS IN GAMES

Visualisation and other forms of representation are widely used techniques to help the general public[1] to personally relate to historical facts and non-fictional accounts. It is possible to read dry scientific books on the history of Scotland. For most people, however, the style of these books is so forbidding that the theme will elude them. They will much more likely get interested in the subject by watching a fictional movie (*Braveheart*), reading a historical novel (Sir Walter Scott's *Rob Roy*) or looking at historical paintings of Bonnie Prince Charlie's flight from Scotland. Where the scientific account only offers the bare facts, visualisation and other forms of representation add flesh to the bone, making their study worthwhile to a broader public.

Fantasy literature, as a rule, is not based on facts nor does it, in its vast majority, take place in the world we know. The worlds it describes and the actions that happen therein most often are only real in the mind of their conceivers and the act of writing fantasy literature in itself is a form of

---

1 In the following, masculine forms imply – where appropriate – feminine ones, too.

representing something that would otherwise not exist outside the writer's imagination. Once an author dies and all his material has been published, the authentic material will only be found in the published text corpus. And yet, as with historical facts, we wish for a deeper knowledge, we wish for more. To satisfy that need, fantasy literature by its very nature as a representation of something that cannot be physically experienced asks more urgently for representation than any other kind of literature.

Profound works such as Tolkien's lead to a multitude of forms of representation as diverse as illustrations, movies, radio adaptations, songs, cartographic works as well as poems and short stories set in Middle-earth, the world he invented. These various forms of representation deal with their subject matter, Tolkien's creation, within the framework of their own capacities and limitations.

One form of representation that is consistently gaining ground these days is games. There have been a few board games, but the main emphasis so far has been on role-playing games. In these games a group of players act as Middle-earth characters and follow game-scenarios under the leadership of a chosen game-master. Iron Crown Entreprises' *Middle-earth Role Playing* series[2] consists of no less than several dozen different game-scenarios. A major part of the characters, events and sites in these role-playing games are found in Tolkien's works. Their description in the published text corpus, however, does not present us with a detailed enough picture to use them in a role-playing game. If we want to play any except the main characters, the game instructions must add a substantial amount of information to what can be found in the text corpus – information that essentially is made up by ICE. But ICE does not stop there. Proceeding from Tolkien's archetypes – sometimes even mere general fantasy archetypes – the role-playing scenarios invent entirely fictitious characters and sites. The game fills up the gaps in Tolkien's creation that the author left to the reader's imagination, thereby offering the players more game options and more fun. The newest

---

[2] Iron Crown Entreprises is henceforth referred to as ICE and *Middle-earth Role Playing* as MERP.

branch of Tolkien-related games, also published by Iron Crown Enterprises, is known under the title of *Middle-earth Collectable Card Game*. It is a card game in which the players aim to achieve a given quest set by the play scenario. The *Middle-earth Collectable Card Game* has been brought to the market with a basic set called *Middle-earth: the Wizards* and two expansion sets, *Middle-earth: the Dragons* and *Middle-earth: Dark Minions*.[3] Although METW is more strictly limited in its actions, METW and MERP have many features in common and they also share a good deal of information that is not derived from the text corpus.

In order to fully achieve its ambitions it is very often not enough for a game to be a true representation of whatever it wants to represent. It must also be fun to play and, mechanically, it must work. These aims can clash and a game may have to divert from what we consider authentic in order to be successful as a game. This is well justified if, otherwise, either the flow of the game is obstructed or the game even does not work at all. It is, however, more difficult to appreciate additions and distortions of this kind if they are not necessary for the game to work. The emphasis of this article will be on the quality of METW as a representation of Tolkien's Middle-earth, even though I am more than willing to make allowances for the benefit of METW as a game.

II MIDDLE-EARTH: THE WIZARDS AS A REPRESENTATION OF TOLKIEN'S WORLD

METW is a card game which consists of five different sorts of cards which can be brought into play to win the game. First of all there are the character cards the player needs to become active in the game. These characters will

---

3 Näf (2004) gives us a final list of expansion sets published, including those published after the initial writing of this article. For practical reasons the scope of this study is limited to *Middle-earth: the Wizards* with occasional digressions to the first two expansion sets. Henceforth the *Middle-earth Collectable Card Game* is referred to as MECCG, *Middle-earth: the Wizards* as METW, *Middle-earth: the Dragons* as METD and *Middle-earth: Dark Minions* as MEDM.

then move around Middle-earth using region and site cards. To further their cause the player may bring into play resource cards while at the same time, to make life (and the game) more interesting, his opponent will also bring in hazard cards that will endanger the player's strategies. This way two or more participants will compete with each other, all of them trying to achieve victory while doing their utmost to deny it to the others.

1. Play Scenarios

1.1 The Original Scenario

The original idea of the game is to find the One Ring and then overcome all the dangers on the way to Mount Doom where the ring shall be destroyed. This is, however, not easily done, so the player first sets out with a small company and hopes to find some useful things that will help him on his way through Middle-earth. Among these things there may be pieces of armour and weaponry, but also palantíri, rings and many other items. He may also bring into play a wizard who from then on will lead the company, find further supporters of his cause and learn many things he may make use of on his quest. If a player achieves the rare feat of finding the One Ring and then even gets it to Mount Doom without losing it or succumbing to its temptations, he is appointed immediate winner of the game once the ring has been destroyed. Most often, however, the prime goal of the scenario is not fully met and then METW offers two alternative ways of appointing the winner of the game.

The first one is applied when all wizards have been brought into play and all but one of the wizards have been eliminated at some stage or other. In this case the player with the sole surviving wizard is the sole remaining player in the game and therefore he has won.

The second alternative is to become the Leader of the Free Council. Under certain conditions the Free Council can be called and the player having acquired most influence, prestige and wisdom (represented by marshalling points) will become its leader. The players can get these marshalling points from the control of characters, resources (allies, items, factions), the destruction of creatures and evil forces, by carrying out the instructions on certain resource cards and avoiding negative points which are accumulated when certain characters the player controls are eliminated.[4]

The original scenario of finding the One Ring, taking it to Mount Doom and destroying it there is taken directly from *The Lord of the Rings*. It is, in a sense, the only scenario that makes sense in the larger context. The only winning condition that ultimately makes sense in this scenario is the destruction of the One Ring as without it every victory is but a temporary victory.

The alternative winning option of acquiring as much influence, prestige and wisdom as possible and thereby overshadowing the other players' achievements also makes some sense in the Tolkien context. In *The Lord of the Rings* there is such a council called the White Council, where the leaders of the West and the wizards come together to discuss their options of thwarting Sauron's plans. As in the game, their standing in the council is also largely connected to their achievements and the wisdom they show.

The other alternative winning option of having the only surviving wizard in play at the end of the game, on the contrary, does not have any such merits. In *The Lord of the Rings*, the corruption or elimination of their fellow wizards is never seen as an aim by the wizards, may they otherwise disagree as much as they want. It is always the wizards' aim to collaborate with one another and at most they will try to make their fellow wizards rally round themselves. One of the primary aims of the game is to gather as many resources as possible against the forces of darkness. Aiming at becoming the sole surviving wizard does not really help towards that purpose. Therefore, hoping for the fellow wizards' elimination should never be an option of winning the game.

Taking into account the many obstacles a company may face if it chooses to go for the One Ring option, the Free Council option looks a good

---

4   ICE (1996:121).

alternative, especially for short games. In longer games, however, the use of the Free Council option should be limited to the very end of the game, when a prolongation of the game is not possible any more. The sole surviving wizard option, on the contrary, should not be applied at all.

In the original scenario of METW, players can win the game in several ways. There is, however, no condition under which all players are considered to be losers. Judged by the text corpus itself this must be seen as a major drawback. If the One Ring had fallen into Sauron's hands, all would have been lost. Therefore there should be an option in the game that, if the company with the bearer of the One Ring is attacked by evil forces and all members are killed, the Ring would fall into Sauron's hands and everything would be lost.[5]

1.2 Other Scenarios suggested for METW

Finding the One Ring and destroying it is not the only interest that can be found in Middle-earth. There is much else that can be done. In its *Middle-earth: the Wizards Companion*[6] ICE has published another eleven scenarios that can be put into practice.

Seven out of the eleven extra scenarios streamline the plot of the game by concentrating the victory conditions on one specific kind of cards. In **Bridge across the Anduin** southern factions must be gathered before Sauron can overrun Gondor, **Fire on Amon Dîn** is a simpler version of this where factions of any kind can be brought together. In **Friends in a Time of Need** it is characters and allies that are central to the plot, whereas in **Council of the Wise** it is rings, and items of any sort in **Heirlooms of the Past**. Rescuing prisoners is the aim in **Barrels out of Bond** and

---

[5] This has basically changed with the publication of the third and fourth expansion sets, *Middle-earth: The Lidless Eye* and *Middle-earth: Against the Shadow*, which allowed combat and interaction between wizard and ringwraith companies.

[6] ICE (1996:59-72).

anything/anybody dwarvish is what counts in **The King beneath the Mountains**. Due to their single-mindedness these scenarios are generally much less fascinating than the original scenario. The only exception to this is **Bridge across the Anduin**, which is made more interesting by the fact that Sauron causes the wizards' working conditions to get worse each turn. Whereas **Bridge across the Anduin**, **Fire on Amon Dîn**, **Friends in a Time of Need** and the **King beneath the Mountains** work quite well as representations of Tolkien's writings, the same cannot be said of the other three scenarios. **Barrels out of Bond**'s sole interest in rescuing prisoners and the **Council of the Wise**'s ring-hunting turn single incidents of *The Lord of the Rings* into major strategies in the struggle against evil. In their single-mindedness they are rather out of touch with the general mood of *The Lord of the Rings*. The same can be said about **Heirlooms of the Past** which suggests wizards running wild in Middle-earth, looking for mighty items that could make the Elvish havens safe from Sauron's onslaught.

There are four scenarios which differ from the simplifying approach mentioned above. Two of them deal with the hobbits. **A Hobbit's Quest** is built on the fact that, from time to time, hobbits went off into the wild seeking adventures. In this scenario they have to accomplish some set tasks and then find their ways back to Bag End. This makes a very interesting task and fits in very well with the atmosphere of Tolkien's writings. **There and Back Again** is a special variety of the scenario mentioned above. It is a solitaire game and loosely follows the plot of *The Hobbit* from Bag End to the Lonely Moutain and back. Its rules are finely tuned to the actions taking place in *The Hobbit* and thereby achieve a remarkable likeness to the book.

The two remaining scenarios are of special interest as the players do not find themselves in a competition for first place only, but in direct confrontation. In the original scenario the players fight for the common good. Although they play hazard cards on their opponents, they do not do this in their own name, but by definition it is Sauron that causes the hazards. The same hazard situation occurs in **A Pilferer at the Prancing Pony**. In addition though, the two players confront each other as one of them steals an item from the other one at the Prancing Pony in Bree. The victim chases the thief throughout Middle-earth to regain his stolen property. In this scenario the actions of the two players take place in direct relation to each other. In view of Tolkien's stories chasing thiefs makes very good sense as a game scenario. It could be especially poignant with Gollum (if he could be made a character) as the victim and Bilbo as the thief. The game mechanics are slightly different with **The Fate of Isildur's Bane**. It is also a game scenario for two persons. One of them plays a wizard who does his best to get the One Ring to Mount Doom where it must be destroyed. His opponent plays Sauron, whose aim is to recapture the ring. Unlike the original scenario, the wizard player can only play resource and character cards and Sauron's player is limited to playing cards that are in the service of darkness. Again their actions are taken in direct relation to each other. The mechanics of **The Fate of Isildur's Bane** represent the dense atmosphere of *The Lord of the Rings* very well. Both scenarios have great qualities as representations of Tolkien's creation and are highly attractive due to the conflict situation between good and evil.

2 The Time-Scheme

METW like any other game with a historical link must have a definite temporal and geographical setting by which its working rules are defined. Such a setting is indispensable as a base from which the players can proceed. Its lack would leave the players virtually in the dark as they would neither know where they are nor what may lie ahead. Whereas the geographical setting of the game is clearly defined as northwestern Middle-earth, the game does not offer any temporal framework. Unlike most games with a historical setting, METW does neither have a clear starting point nor a fixed time frame. The main information we get about the temporal setting of the game comes from the introduction to the game and the cards it is made up of.

In the introduction to the game[7] we are told that five wizards had once come to Middle-earth to unite the forces of good so that Sauron could be thwarted in his attempt to seize absolute power over Middle-earth. This was achieved for good after a long and hardy struggle by the destruction of the One Ring. We find time indications for these events in the Tale of Years in *The Lord of the Rings*[8]. For the coming of the five wizards to Middle-earth the year 1000 of the Third Age serves as a rough time reference, whereas the destruction of the One Ring is set at 3019. The introduction to the game does not offer us any precise starting point, it can only be inferred that it must lie somewhere between the years 1000 and 3019 of the Third Age.

We can only get a clearer picture about the time-scheme of the game from the set of characters that can be brought into play and the resources and hazards that can be mustered. The analysis of the card evidence points to the end of the Third Age. It is, however, impossible to fix the exact period of time in this most turbulent part of the age. Even if we only take the character cards into consideration, the evidence is not clear and two different periods of the history of the Third Age suggest themselves. The main set of characters dates from the period of the War of the Rings, i.e. 3018-19 Third Age, but then again we find some characters that have died long before 3018, as is mentioned in the Tale of Years[9]. The main example is Thorin II Oakenshield who died at the Battle of the Five Armies in 2941, other examples we find in Bard the Bowman who can be assumed to have died in 2977 and Balin of Thorin's company who died in Moria in 2994. Of the thirteen dwarves in Thorin's company only seven were still alive in 3018.[10] If we, however, take Thorin II and his company as acting characters, we find ourselves at the time of the Quest of Erebor which took place at around 2941. In this case we would have to do without Frodo (born 2968), his younger cousins Merry and Pippin, Sam Gamgee and also many more

---

7   ICE (1995:2).
8   Tolkien (1981c:457, 472).
9   Tolkien (1981c:464f).
10 Tolkien (1981a:300f, 416-419).

characters such as Éowyn and Éomer who were not yet born at the time of the Quest of Erebor.[11] As we can see, the time-scheme of the game is not clearly defined and card evidence can be found both in favour of and against the two periods of time mentioned above.

An unclear time-scheme is a drawback in a game that is based on history, but in itself this would not pose a major problem, were there some rules ensuring that the cards could only be played in the right context. In METW, however, there are no such rules and it can happen that both Bard the Bowman and Éowyn appear simultaneously on stage, a very unlikely event as Bard the Bowman died of old age 18 years before Éowyn was born.

How can these time discrepancies be dealt with? On the one hand, history is a chronological one-way system. Once an event has taken place, it cannot be undone any more. On the other hand, however, every event may lead to a big variety of alternative actions. The sequence of events in Tolkien's works is but one of many which could have happened at the time. History could equally have taken different turns at various moments in time. Gandalf might, for example, not have met Thorin II on his way to the Shire or he might have failed in persuading him to launch a secret attack on Smaug with the help of twelve followers and a "rather greedy and fat"[12] hobbit named Bilbo. Thorin II, as a consequence, might then have made his dreams of a great military campaign against the dragon come true, with the annihilation of the dwarves as a military and political factor in Middle-earth as a likely outcome. Or he might as well have done nothing and bided his time with the result that he would have got much older than he actually did. This would, of course, have changed the whole history of Middle-earth and as a result even Thorin and Frodo might have met in Rivendell to form an alliance under one of the five wizards, although it is quite hard to imagine what Frodo would have done there, had he not inherited the One Ring from his uncle Bilbo.

---

11 Tolkien (1981c:465, 478-482).
12 Tolkien (1982:321-323).

In theory this idea of parallel historical options works fine and an outcome such as the meeting of Thorin II and Frodo in Rivendell is not impossible. I doubt, however, that such a course of action would be probable. Even if Thorin II had grown to a much older age than he did and met Frodo in Rivendell, he would not have been fit enough to go orc-ahunting any more. The characters we find in the game do not always co-exist with each other and the same can be said about the resources they may take advantage of or the hazards that might befall them. Discrepancies remain that simply will not be explained away under any circumstances, and this is one of the weak points in METW as an adaptation of Tolkien's world.

Another negative side effect of this missing time frame is, that it is much harder to judge the quality with which Tolkien's stories have been adapted for gaming. Some aspects of the story are very well translated into the game if we take 2941 as the starting point, but they are not if we have 3018 in mind. With other aspects the opposite is true. This way a clear-cut analysis of the relationship between the contents of the cards and the rules of the game on the one hand and the reality of Middle-earth on the other is very difficult to achieve.

3 The Geography

A game with historical links does not only need a set chronological time frame for things to happen, it also needs a clearly defined space where they can take place. When it comes to geography, METW is highly successful in making Tolkien's world come true.

METW offers two different kinds of cards to represent the geography of Middle-earth: region cards and site cards. The two sorts of cards have different functions in the game. The region cards represent larger geographical and geopolitical entities. They are mainly in the game to monitor the characters' movements. The site cards, in contrast, represent local focus points – either places of great importance or places which are typical of a certain region. Whereas the regions are there to move through, the sites are the places where actions take place.

3.1 The Regions of Middle-earth

METW takes place in the northwestern part of Middle-earth, where also the events of *The Lord of the Rings* and *The Hobbit* are based. To achieve movement of similar speed the northwest of Middle-earth is divided up into 52 geographical regions, five of which are sea and the remaining 47 land areas.

The division of Eriador, the land west of the Misty Mountains, into 13 regions generally fits in well with Tolkien's writing. The biggest part of Eriador once belonged to the mannish kingdom of Arnor with its three regional entities called Arthedain, Rhudaur and Cardolan. Whereas the game follows Tolkien in the cases of Rhudaur and Cardolan, Arthedain, due to its size, has been split into three regions: the ethnically defined Shire of the Hobbits, Arthedain and Númeriador. For the latter no evidence can be found in Tolkien, nor is there any reason to believe that it is much different from the rest of the former kingdom. The creation of Númeriador[13] is due rather to the need of cutting up Arthedain for movement reasons than to Middle-earth evidence. We find ethnically defined areas in the Elvish costal province of Lindon, the Shire, Forochel, Dunland and in Hollin. Angmar and Enedwaith also are distinct areas in Middle-earth and rightly form regions of their own in the game. We encounter more difficulties with the land once inhabited by the Drúedain. In the game it is split up into two regions, the Old Pûkel-land and the Old Pûkel Gap. In Tolkien no evidence is found of such a gap in the White Mountains. For this reason the region of the Old Pûkel Gap would better have been included either in the Old Pûkel-

---

13 The name of the region is interesting, though. It is made up of *númen* (west) and *Eriador*, a similar morphological phenomenon as found in *Eredain* (from *ered* (mountains) and *edain* (men), name of the Swiss Tolkien Society) and *Aglared* (from *agla* (beautiful) and *ered*, name of the Swiss Tolkien Society fanzine).

land or the White Mountains.[14] A further two small errors can be found in the map of Eriador. The first one is the extension of Enedwaith stretching as far east as the Gap of Isen, claiming land that in Tolkien belonged to Dunland. The second problem concerns Angmar. In METW Angmar lies to the north of the Misty Mountains, whereas Tolkien states that the evil kingdom of Angmar lies on both sides of the Misty Mountains.[15] The Misty Mountains should therefore not wedge in between Angmar and Rhudaur, but rather between southern and northern Angmar.

The Misty Mountains form a most remarkable barrier to movement from Eriador to Wilderland. In METW we find only two crossing points, the High Pass and the Redhorn Gate. Long detours can lead around them in the south by the Gap of Isen and in the north by Angmar and Gundabad. This fits well in with Tolkien's description of Middle-earth. East of the Misty Mountains we find the Anduin Vales and further south Wold & Foothills, Fangorn and Rohan. Between the mountains and the river only the Wold & Foothills pose a problem as this region consists of two distinct areas, the wild and uninhabited Wold and the highly populated and well fortified woodland realm of Lórien. The creation of two regions would have been preferable in Middle-earth context. Further east the huge forest of Mirkwood is split into four regions, two of which are politically defined. The first one is Southern Mirkwood under the control of Dol Guldur, the second one the Woodland Realm under the Elvish king Thranduil. The two middle regions, on the contrary, were created to cut up the remaining forest for movement reasons rather than for Tolkien evidence. The same applies to Northern and Southern Rhovanion which form an ethnic and political entity. The remaining areas of Wilderland, i.e. the Grey Mountain Narrows, the

---

14 The region cards of the Old Pûkel Gap and Andrast suggest an extension of the White Mountains, which renders movement between Andrast and the Old Pûkel Gap impossible. This is, however, as questionable as the extension of the southern range of the Blue Mountains, which – according to the relevant region cards – separates Lindon from Cardolan.

15 ICE (1996:2 (color insert)); Tolkien (1981c:389).

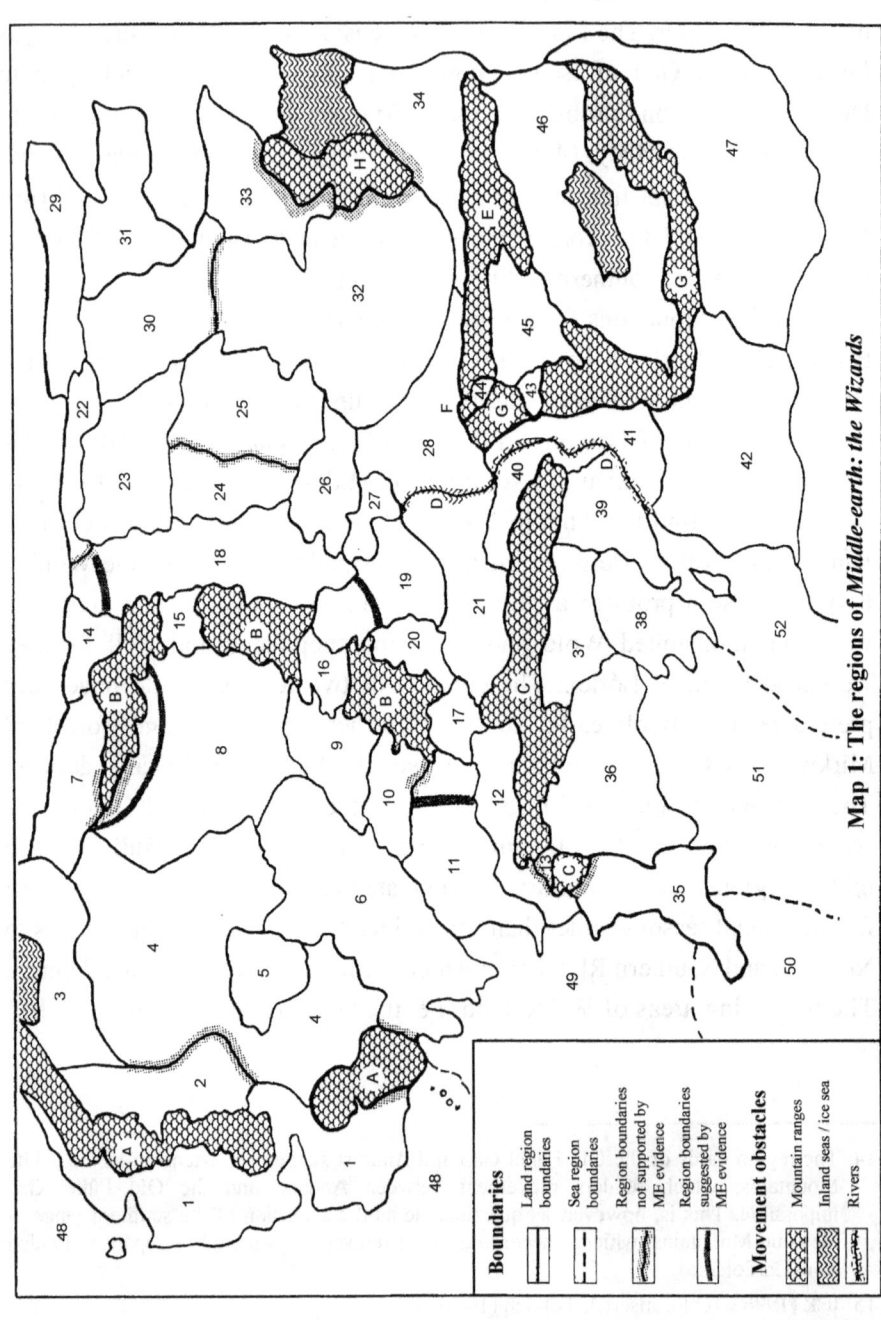

Map 1: The regions of *Middle-earth: the Wizards*

The regions of Middle-earth: the Wizards

1 Lindon
2 Númeriador
3 Forochel
4 Arthedain
5 The Shire
6 Cardolan
7 Angmar
8 Rhudaur
9 Hollin
10 Dunland
11 Enedwaith
12 Old Púkel-land
13 Old Púkel Gap
14 Gundabad
15 High Pass
16 Redhorn Gate
17 Gap of Isen
18 Anduin Vales
19 Wold & Foothills
20 Fangorn
21 Rohan
22 Grey Mountain Narrows
23 Woodland Realm
24 Western Mirkwood
25 Heart of Mirkwood
26 Southern Mirkwood
27 Brown Lands
28 Dagorlad
29 Withered Heath
30 Northern Rhovanion
31 Iron Hills
32 Southern Mirkwood
33 Dorwinion
34 Horse Plains
35 Andrast
36 Anfalas
37 Lamedon
38 Belfalas
39 Lebennin
40 Anórien
41 Ithilien
42 Harondor
43 Imlad Morgul
44 Udûn
45 Gorgoroth
46 Nurn
47 Khand
48 Elven Shores
49 Eriadoran Coast
50 Andrast Coast
51 Bay of Belfalas
52 Mouths of the Anduin

Movement obstacles

A Blue Mountains
B Misty Mountains
C White Mountains
D Anduin River
E Ash Mountains
F Morannon
G Mountains of Shadow
H Mountains at the Sea of Rhûn

Iron Hills, Dorwinion, the Brown Lands, Dagorlad and the Horse Plains, are all well chosen from geographical and political viewpoints and of all the regional names only the Horse Plains has no basis in Tolkien. The boundaries of the Wilderland regions are well set with the exception of the northernmost part of the Anduin Vales which wedges in between Mount Gundabad and the Grey Mountain Narrows. The northern end of the Anduin Vales region should rather have been made a part of the Grey Mountain Narrows linking the two areas of darkness.

The regions of Gondor and Mordor are, geographically and politically, much better defined than the northern lands, which made the internal division of the two realms much easier. As a consequence, these regions please even the purists among Tolkien readers. The only slight criticism that could be voiced concerns the omission of Umbar which should have been included in a comprehensive game on Middle-earth.

The division of the sea into five regions mainly serves the purpose of bringing sea travel into line with movement over land. This division is, however, not arbitrary, as the boundaries of the sea regions closely follow geographical and ethnic criteria.

Middle-earth consists of a patchwork of regions, which generally allows travels to take place between neighbouring regions. There are, however, also some obstacles which force almost all traffic to make long detours. Most important in this are mountain ranges. In the far west we find such an obstacle in the Blue Mountains, which renders direct movement between Lindon and Forochel impossible. A much greater impediment are the Misty Mountains. Direct movement between Eriador and Wilderland is only possible through the High Pass, the Redhorn Gate or by some long detour far to the south or far to the north. Likewise the White Moutains act as an impediment between Gondor on the one hand and Eriador and Wilderland respectively on the other. We find further obstacles with the Ash Mountains and the Mountains of Shadow, which wall off Mordor from its neighbouring regions. METW[16] has introduced another mountain range west of the Sea of Rhûn, which renders travels between Dorwinion and the Horse Plains impossible. This mountain range can also be found on the map to *The Lord of the Rings*. Its size, however, does not warrant its inclusion as an obstacle in METW.

Direct movement across these mountain ranges is not possible unless the moving company includes a ranger and can play a resource card allowing the ranger to find a direct way through the mountains. Such cards are available for all mountain ranges except the Blue Mountains and the mountains west of the Sea of Rhûn. Mountains are an important element in Tolkien's plots and therefore they rightly belong to the game as factors opposing movement. This and the fact that rangers can find their way through them must be seen as positive features of the game. Two further obstacles can be found in METW. The first one is the River Anduin south of Wold & Foothills and the Brown Lands. Direct movement across the river except between Anórien and Ithilien is only possible if the company includes a ranger and can play the appropriate resource card[17]. The second obstacle is the Morannon, which separates Dagorlad from Udûn. Only a small company, including a scout, can try to sneak through playing the appropriate resource card.

The regions in Middle-earth differ greatly in relation to their civilization and danger levels. METW aims at representing these differences by keying specific events or dangers to individual regions or, more often, to sets of regions classified according to their civilization and danger levels. The classification system METW[18] uses is based on six region types with the following general characteristics:

---

16 ICE (1996:2 (color insert)).

17 The card also mentions the possibility of movement between Anórien and Ithilien, although there is no impediment of movement there in the first place. This must have been an oversight on the part of ICE.

18 ICE (1996:21).

- Coastal Seas: regions consisting of coastal seas and open water. They may also include islands. Travelling through coastal sea areas is not wrought with too many dangers.
- Free-domains: very safe, highly civilized regions where only few hazards may befall travellers.
- Border-lands: fortified regions on the border of wilderness or shadow territories. They are relatively safe to travel.
- Wildernesses: sparsely populated, uncivilized regions. Due to the lack of political and military control these territories are open ground for surprise attacks.
- Shadow-lands: regions with some active shadow-forces and settlements. Sauron's forces generally have higher ground in these areas. Travelling through these areas is very dangerous.
- Dark-domains: regions with heavy concentration of shadow-forces. There are only small chances of survival in these areas.

The region type classification system permits an accurate classification of the regions according to their civilization and danger levels. The quality of the representation of Middle-earth mostly depends on the classification of the individual regions.

With the exception of three regions, METW classifies all of Eriador as wilderness. The only exceptions are the Elvish region of Lindon and the Hobbits' Shire, which belong to the free-domains, and Angmar, a shadow-land.

Wilderland is perceived as much more varied. There are no free-domains in Wilderland, but the border-lands of the Gap of Isen, Rohan, Anduin Vales, Woodland Realm and the wine-growing country of Dorwinion give the forces of good a strong basis to start from. The forces of darkness have their strongholds, too, though. Dark-domains are found in Southern Mirkwood and Gundabad, and the barren regions bordering Dol Guldur and Mordor (Brown Lands, Dagorlad, Horse Plains) are classified as shadow-lands. The remaining ten regions are wilderness areas again.

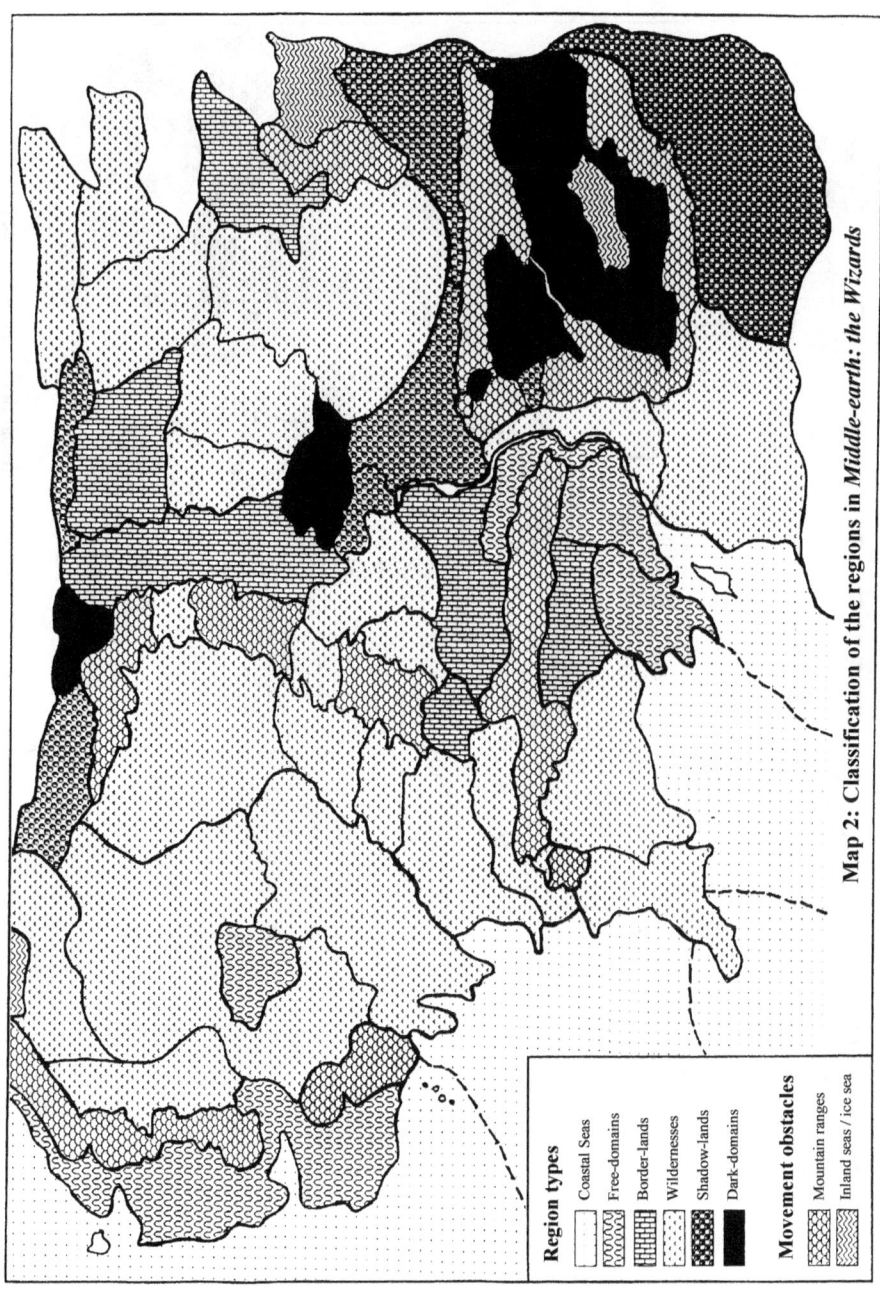

Map 2: Classification of the regions in *Middle-earth: the Wizards*

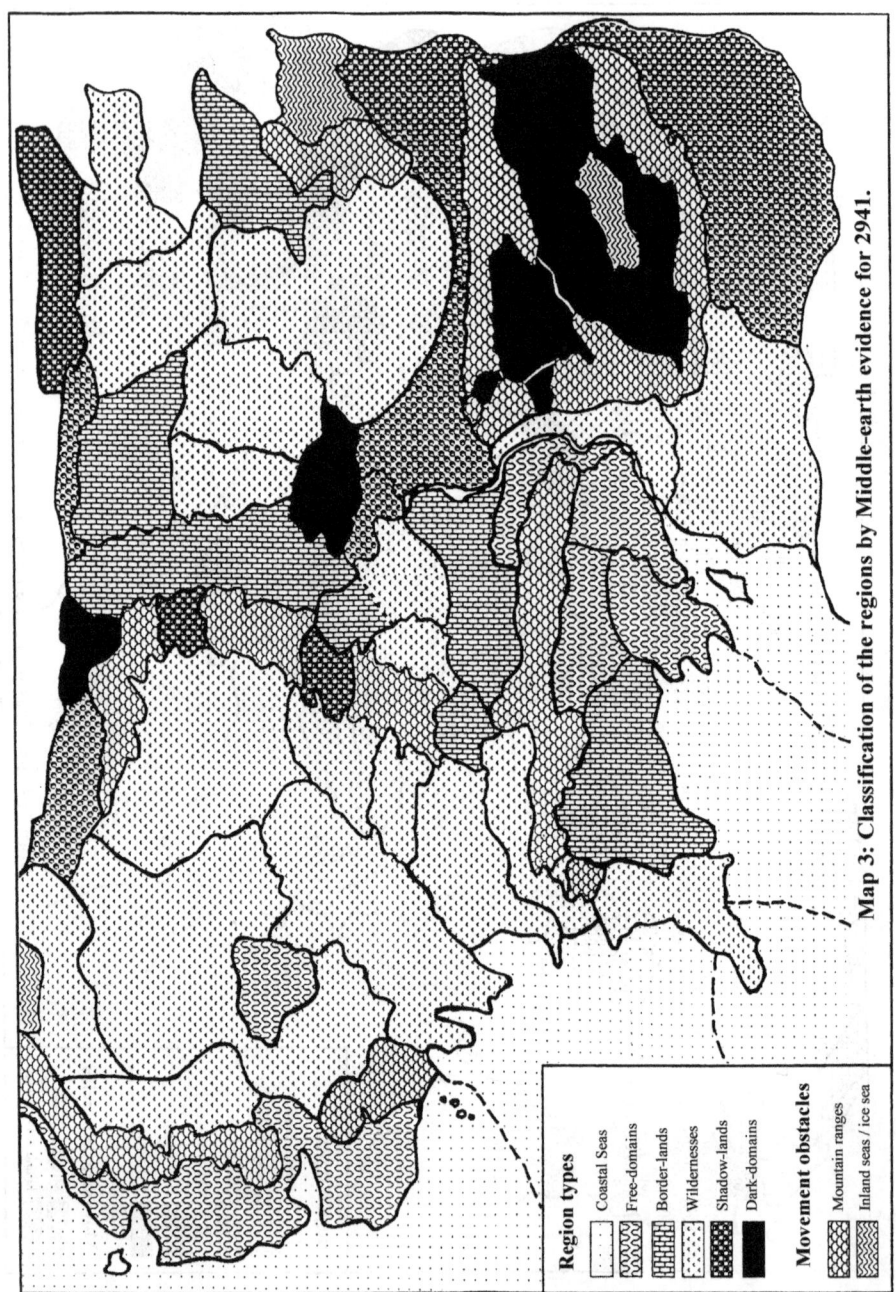

Map 3: Classification of the regions by Middle-earth evidence for 2941.

Middle-earth: The Wizards – The Representation of Tolkien's World in the Game 123

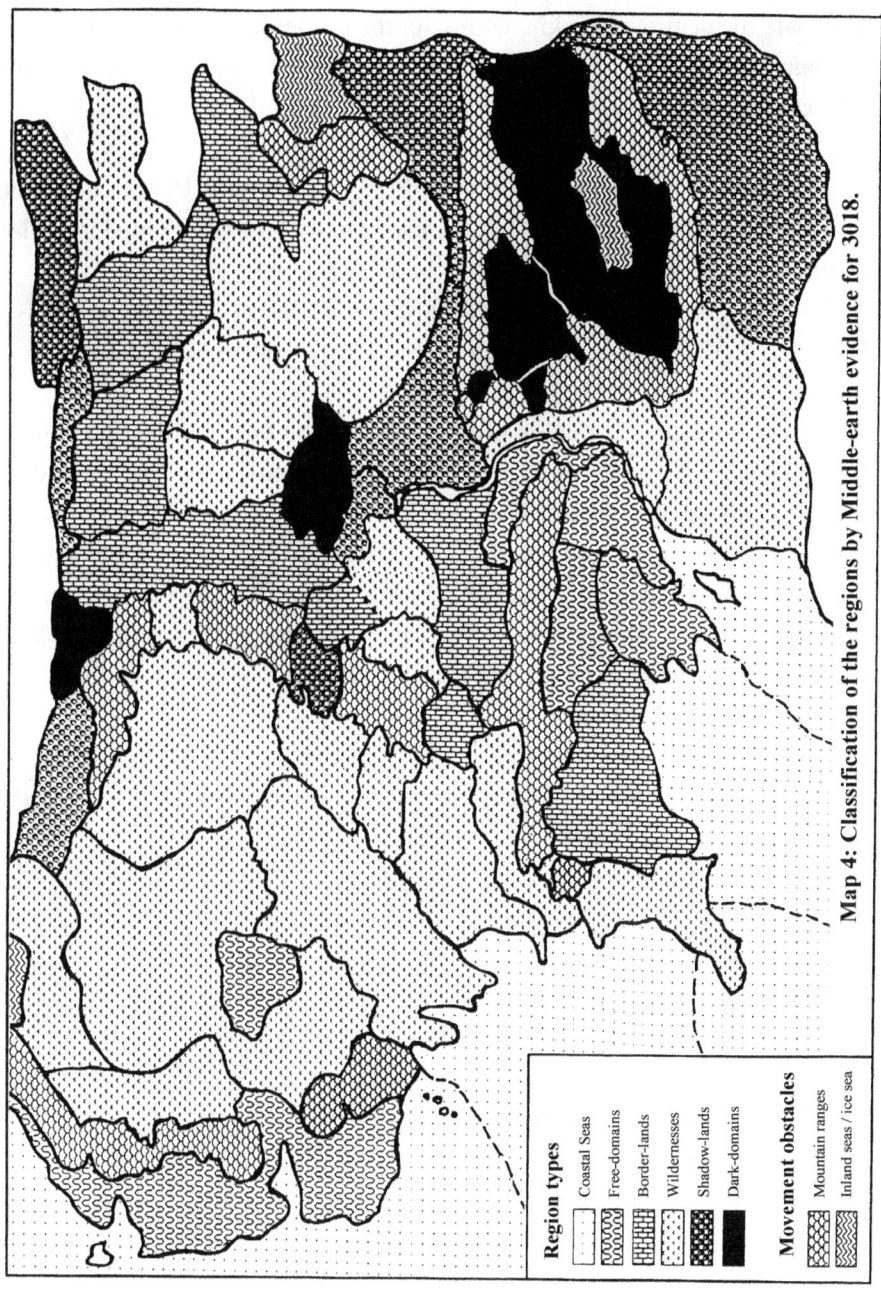

Map 4: Classification of the regions by Middle-earth evidence for 3018.

Gondor is clearly the core area of the forces of good. Free-domains dominate the centre of the kingdom with the border-land Lamedon covering it against the western wilderness areas of Anfalas and Andrast. We find further wilderness areas in Ithilien and Harondor bordering the dark areas of Mordor.

Mordor is the centre of evil. The three core regions of Udûn, Gorgoroth and Nurn are dark-domains whereas the regions bordering Gondor, Imlad Morgul and Khand, are considered to be shadow-lands.

The sea areas are all classified as coastal seas, as the danger level is judged to be the same in all the sea areas of northwestern Middle-earth.

If we want to judge the quality of the classification of the individual regions in METW, we run into one big methodical problem, namely the messed up time-scheme of the game. The classification of a specific region as a wilderness may make good sense for the time of the Quest of Erebor, but the same might not be the case at the time of the War of the Ring or the other way round. The only way we can do justice to this problem is by comparing the classification in METW with the situation during both periods mentioned above.

The literary evidence we find in Tolkien points to a classification of the regions of Eriador which is identical with the one in METW for both the time of the Quest of Erebor and the War of the Ring.

We get a different picture for the regions of Wilderland. The situation during the Quest of Erebor was markedly darker than is shown in METW. The crossing of the Misty Mountains was highly threatened by concentrated shadow-forces and shadow-settlements such as the Goblin-town mentioned in *The Hobbit* in the High Pass region and Moria with its orc-settlement, the Balrog and the Watcher in the Water at the Redhorn Gate. Both crossings were rather shadow-lands than wildernesses in 2941. The same applies to the Withered Heath with its high concentration of dragon lairs. A profound change of the strategic situation was brought about by the death of Smaug, the destruction of large forces of orcs and the stabilization of regional power-centres of the Free Peoples in northeastern and northwestern

Wilderland. The Redhorn Gate, which was less affected by the outcome of the Quest of Erebor, was still a shadow-land. The High Pass, on the contrary, lost some of its terror and for 3018 it is aptly classified as a wilderness. Further east, the Withered Heath remained a shadow-land, but Northern Rhovanion came under the combined control of the dwarves of the Lonely Mountains, the men of Dale and the elves from Thranduil's Halls. In 3018, Northern Rhovanion was more of a border-land than a wilderness. The remaining regions of Wilderland are aptly classified in METW, whichever historical period we have in mind. We face a special problem with the region Wold & Foothills. Whereas the Wold was a wilderness in both periods, Lórien can only be classified as a border-land. The creation of two regions instead of one would have been a great advantage to the game as it would have allowed a more accurate representation of this part of Middle-earth.

The literary evidence also differs from METW in the case of Gondor, which was quite safer both in 2941 and 3018 than the region classifications would make one believe. Not only Arnórien, Lebennin and Belfalas should have been classified as free-domains, but also Lamedon, which in the game is treated as a border-land. Anfalas finally was more of a border-land than a wilderness.

Mordor, on the contrary, gets away too well. Imlad Morgul is classified as a shadow-land, although the heavy concentration of Nazgûls, orc-fortresses such as Minas Morgul and Cirith Ungol and the monster spider Shelob testify to its inherent darkness. Classification as a dark-domain would have been more adequate.

The identical classification of all sea areas is highly compatible with Middle-earth reality as no difference can be discerned in the way the individual sea areas were protected by Ulmo, Lord of Waters, against the forces of darkness.

The region classification of METW is appropriate in 45.5 out of 52 cases for both the time of the Quest of Erebor and the War of the Ring. We find a difference between the historical analysis and METW in only 6.5 cases for each period out of which 5.5 are identical for the two periods. The messed-up time-scheme is of little importance when it comes to the classification of the regions. Only in two cases a difference is found between 2941 and 3018. Whereas METW more closely resembles the situation of 2941 in the case of Northern Rhovanion, it fits in better with 3018 in the case of the High Pass. The representation of the regions in METW is a positive asset to the game.

3.2 The Sites of Middle-earth

Whereas companies move through regions, it is the sites they are really interested in. There they can find the supporters, allies and items which will help them to overcome the forces of darkness.

METW offers the players 69 sites to travel to. Among them we find cities and towns such as Minas Tirith, Minas Morgul or Bree, but also important locations in the wilderness such as Amon Hen, Henneth Annûn or single towers and houses such as Isengard, a Ruined Signal Tower in Enedwaith or Beorn's House. The sites can be centres of cultural and political importance or ruins of lost cultures such as Ost-in-Edhil in formerly Elvish Hollin. METW also includes two sites which would make more sense as regions. One of them is Lórien which could feature Caras Galadhon as its site, the other one is Tolfalas.

The sites are not evenly distributed throughout Middle-earth. The amount of sites in a region is most strongly linked to the importance the region has in Tolkien's writings. Prominent regions tend to feature several sites, whereas regions which are but peripheral in *The Hobbit* and *The Lord of the Rings* are lucky to get at least one site. The first group includes Arthedain, Rhudaur, the Anduin Vales, Rohan, the Withered Heath[19] and Imlad Morgul which all offer 3 sites each. Udûn, Nurn, Southern Rhovanion and the sea-regions of Andrast Coast and the Bay of Belfalas which do not

---

19 The Withered Heath comes as a bit of a surprise in this context as it does not feature too prominently in either *The* Hobbit or *The Lord of the Rings*. The same can be said about Angmar and Forochel which have got no less than two sites in METW. The game includes these sites in order to increase the options of the game.

have any sites at all are found in the second group.[20] There is a fair number of regions which are of little prominence in Tolkien's books. Most often his writings give only very limited information about them, if any at all. As ICE wanted to include these areas in the game, too, it had to create sites which do not exist in Tolkien's writings. Of the 69 sites in METW, 46 are mentioned in Tolkien's books; the other 23, however, have been invented by ICE. In order to create sites ICE used two different methods.

The first method consists in defining sites ethnologically rather than geographically. A prime example of this is the Easterling Camp. From Tolkien's books we know that a people called Easterlings lived in tents on the plain north of the Ash Mountains. We do not know where exactly they lived, but the inclusion of an Easterling Camp on the Horse Plains in METW fits in well with literary evidence. The ethnological approach is highly consistent with Tolkien's work and his concept of sub-creation. Its only limitation lies in the consistency of the invented facts with literary evidence. Of the fifteen sites created this way, all but two, Lossadan Cairn and the Stones, seem plausible.

The second method of inventing sites does not limit itself to representing ethnic populations. It pretends to offer sites, which are geographically as clearly defined as the ones taken from Tolkien. These sites have definite place names and thus make people believe that there is some Middle-earth evidence of their existence. A good example of this approach is Irerock, a dragon lair in the Withered Heath. Tolkien himself mentioned dragons in the northern wastes, but never explained where they lived. METW could have included such dragon lairs by using general place names, but instead they went for specific ones. This method, which was used in eight cases, is not above suspicion as it makes those players who have not come into

---

20 With the expansions sets of METD and MEDM a further 22 sites are introduced with the result that Southern Rhovanion, Nurn and Andrast Coast have finally got sites, too. Only Udûn and Bay of Belfalas have still not got any sites.

contact with the 'real thing' believe that these sites are part of Tolkien's sub-creation, which clearly they are not.[21]

This creation of new sites is taking place while the game is forgetting all about some others which are of considerable importance to Middle-earth history. Prime examples of this oversight are the ruins of Annúminas, Fornost and Osgiliath, the city of Linhir, haunted Dwimorberg, the Carrock and the orc stronghold of Durthang. As a representation of Tolkien's world METW would have fared much better by including sites like Osgiliath than by featuring others for which no literary evidence can be found.

The geographical positioning of the sites in METW is but crudely done by naming the regions they are supposed to lie in. Taking the 46 sites into account for which we have Middle-earth evidence, the quality of the representation is very high, as agreement is fine in all but four cases. We get a first dubious case in Amon Hen, which according to METW is set in Rohan. Historically, though, Amon Hen has always been a part of Gondor. Its inclusion in Rohan can only be defended on purely geographical grounds. Clearer still is the case of the Glittering Caves, which are set in the Gap of Isen, but both geographically and politically have always belonged to the kingdom of the Rohirrim. We find a similar situation in Rhosgobel, which is set in Southern Mirkwood, but in the *Fellowship of the Ring* is said to be "near the borders of Mirkwood"[22], i.e. within the boundaries of the Anduin Vales. The last deviation is found in the Isles of the Dead that Live, which according to METW is set in the Eriadoran Coast. Fonstad's maps[23] of Beleriand in the First Age and on the changes of Arda at the beginning of the Second Age, however, point to a position in the prolongation of the southern Blue Mountains, i.e. in the region of the Elven Shores.

---

21 The same method is used extensively in ICE's Middle-earth role-playing modules, which partly explains their mixed reception in Tolkien circles.

22 Tolkien (1981a:336). This view is adopted by Fonstad (1992:76 & 80) and J.E.A. Tyler (1979:488).

23 Fonstad (1992:13 & 38). The gamemakers weakened their own position in ICE (1996:3 (color insert)) by setting the Isles of the Dead that Live within the Elven Shores.

Like the regions, the sites have also got a classification system based on their civilization and danger levels. It consists of the following six site types.

- Havens: highly safe sites of rest and healing. No danger can befall companies at havens.
- Free-holds: safe sites, no automatic-attacks against visiting companies, only few hazards can be played against them.
- Border-holds: sites of relative safety, no automatic-attacks on visiting companies, considerably more hazards can be played than at free-holds.
- Ruins and Lairs: deserted sites, inhabited by dangerous creatures which will automatically attack visiting companies. Additionally a minor number of middle-quality hazards can be played against them.
- Shadow-holds: relatively deserted sites, inhabited by dangerous creatures which will automatically attack visiting companies (exception: Mount Doom). Also a fair number of the high-quality hazards can attack there.
- Dark-holds: very dangerous sites with heavy concentrations of shadow-forces, which will automatically attack visiting companies. In addition hazards of the worst kind including Nazgûls can be played. The chances of surviving a visit at a dark-hold are low as not only the quality of hazards but also the odds in favour of playing them are extremely high.

The site type classification system permits an accurate classification of the sites according to their civilization and danger levels. Here again the quality of the representation of Middle-earth mostly depends on the classification of the individual sites.

The only four havens in METW are Edhellond, the Grey Havens, Lórien and Rivendell, the strongholds of Elvish culture in Middle-earth. Their military and magic defence as well as the Elves' relative immunity from the temptation of evil sets them apart from the other sites.

Whereas free and border-holds are introduced as distinct site types, the dividing line between the individual sites classified unter the two labels is

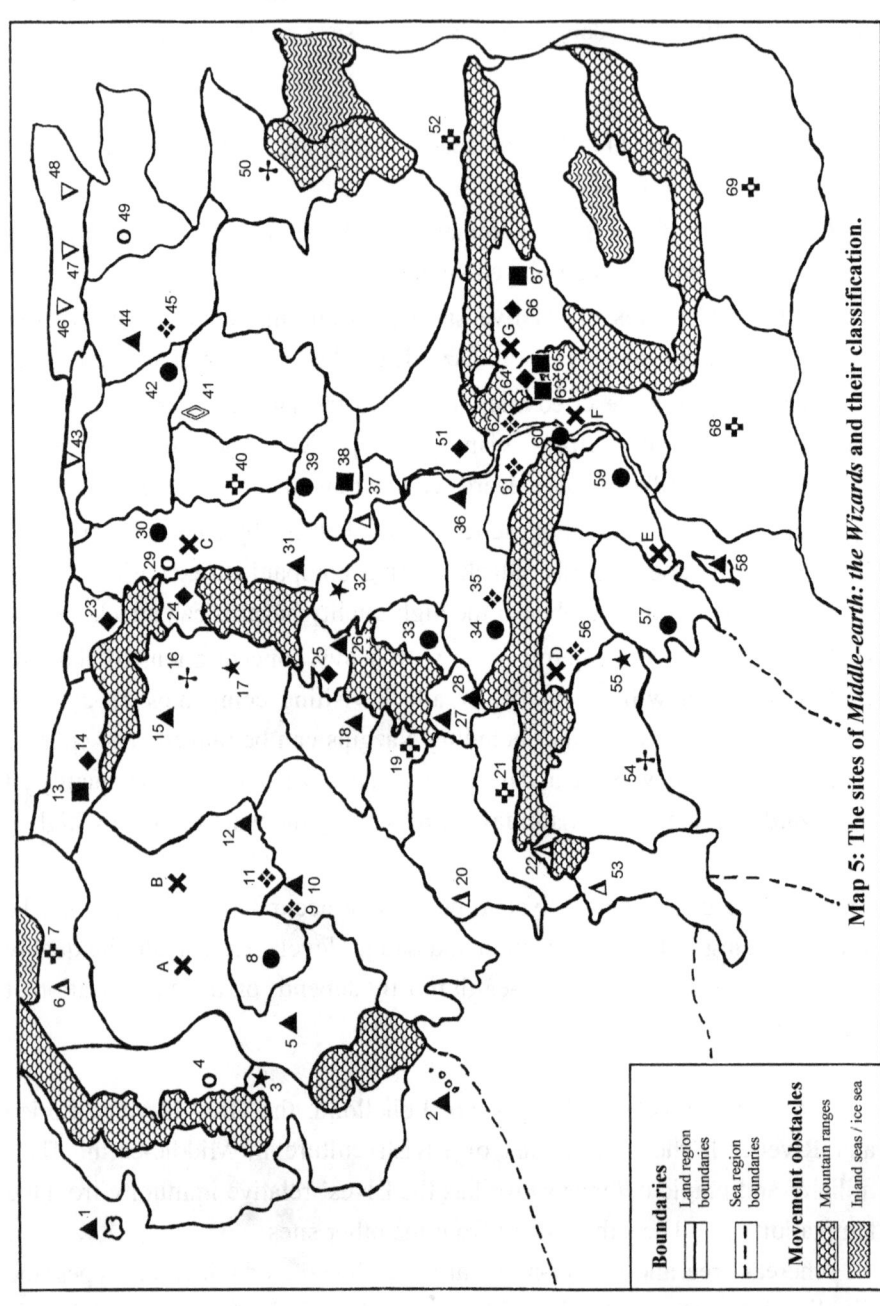

Map 5: The sites of *Middle-earth: the Wizards* and their classification.

Middle-earth: The Wizards – The Representation of Tolkien's World in the Game 131

Sites included in *Middle-earth: the Wizards*

1. Himring
2. Isles of the Dead that Live
3. Grey Havens
4. Blue Mountain Dwarf-hold
5. The White Towers
6. Lossadan Cairn
7. Lossadan Camp
8. Bag End
9. Old Forest
10. Barrow-downs
11. Bree
12. Weathertop
13. Carn Dûm
14. Mount Gram
15. Ettenmoors
16. Cameth Brin
17. Rivendell
18. Ost-in-Edhil
19. Dunnish Clan-hold
20. Ruined Signal Tower
21. Wose Passage-hold
22. Stone-Circle
23. Mount Gundabad
24. Goblin-gate
25. Moria
26. Dimrill Dale
27. Isengard
28. Glittering Caves
29. Eagles' Eyrie
30. Beorn's House
31. Gladden Fields
32. Lórien
33. Wellinghall
34. Edoras
35. Dunharrow
36. Amon Hen
37. Bandit Lair
38. Dol Guldur
39. Rhosgobel
40. Woodmen-town
41. Sarn Goriwing
42. Thranduil's Halls
43. The Wind Throne
44. The Lonely Mountain
45. Lake-town
46. Dancing Spire
47. Irerock
48. Caves of Úlund
49. Iron Hill Dwarf-hold
50. Shrel-Kain
51. Dead Marshes
52. Easterling Camp
53. The Stones
54. Lond Galen
55. Edhellond
56. Vale of Erech
57. Dol Amroth
58. Tolfalas
59. Pelargir
60. Minas Tirith
61. Drúadan Forest
62. Henneth Annûn
63. Minas Morgul
64. Shelob's Lair
65. Cirith Ungol
66. Mount Doom
67. Barad-dûr
68. Southron Oasis
69. Variag Camp

Sites not included in METW

A. Annúminas
B. Fornost
C. The Carrock
D. Dwimorberg
E. Linhir
F. Osgiliath
G. Durthang

Keys to the map

	Havens	Free-holds	Border-holds	Ruins and Lairs	Shadow-holds	Dark-holds
Sites taken from Tolkien	★	●	❖	◀	◆	■
Sites invented by ICE (ethnol. defined)		○	♣	◁	◇	
Sites invented by ICE (geogr. defined)			✠	▽		
Sites not included in METW	✗	✗	✗	✗	✗	✗

not always clear. Some sites clearly fit one of these two types. Others however, like Beorn's House, Edoras, Thranduil's Halls, the Dwarf-holds (all free-holds), Lond Galen, the Vale of Erech and Woodmen-town (all border-holds) could be classified either way. Of the 29 free and border-holds, all but seven clearly belong to this site type continuum. Four of them – the Dunnish Clan-hold, the Easterling and Variag Camps and the Southron Oasis – have been included in METW to make factions available which, in Tolkien's books, are seen as more than potentially hostile. They would make rather better sense as shadow-holds. Doubtful, too, are Rhosgobel – Radagast's temporary home-place –, which lies too close to Barad-dûr and lacks sufficient protection to be counted among the free-holds, and the Old Forest, which features both good and evil in the persons of Tom Bombadil, Goldberry and Old Man Willow. The last one, Eagle's Eyrie, does not really fit any site type.

Of the ruins and lairs most are not inhabited and all of them are devoid of any political or military control – be it of good or evil. We find among them former centres of political, military and cultural importance, desolate places and lairs of dangerous creatures and bandits. There are no less than 23 such sites and all but four of them fit in well with the definition. The first one, the White Towers, was still manned by elves in the War of the Ring and should have been included as a border-hold.[24] The same classification should have been applied to Isengard, Saruman's fortress, and Tolfalas, a Gondorean Island. The Lonely Mountain, finally, could equally well be classified in three categories, as a lair or a shadow-hold in 2941 or as a border-hold in 3018.

Once again, the dividing line between shadow and dark-holds cannot be drawn as clearly as might be wished. Barad-dûr, Dol Guldur, Minas Morgul are true dark-holds, being ruled by Sauron himself or by one of his closest followers. There are, however, a couple of sites like Moria, Goblin-gate, Mount Gram, Mount Gundabad (shadow-holds), Carn Dûm and Cirith Ungol (dark-holds), which could equally well be classified as either of the

---

24 Tolkien (1981a:349).

two site types. Of the 13 shadow and dark-holds all but one – the Dead Marshes, which is more of a ruin and lair – rightly belong to this site type continuum.

The representation of Middle-earth sites generally is of good quality as of the 69 sites no more than 4 are definitely put into the wrong category. There are, however, major transition zones between all neighbouring site types from the free-holds up to the dark-holds and even between the border and the shadow-holds. This points to some vagueness with which the site type classification system was applied to the sites. In addition it illustrates the general problem of applying a rigorous classification system to reality.

The classification of a site does not only have an influence on the hazards that can be played, but also on the resources. Characters, allies and factions in general are only playable at havens, free-holds and border-holds. The only exceptions to this are Gollum, Saruman and partly Roäc the Raven.[25] This fits in well with Middle-earth evidence as havens, free and border-holds are sites of relative safety, places where friends of the Free Peoples can be met. This is much less the case with ruins and lairs or shadow and dark-holds.

Items, on the contrary, are much more likely to be found at places where companies can only get to by taking risks, i.e. ruins and lairs, shadow and dark-holds. With the exception of a very few items which are keyed to specific sites or site types, they cannot be played at havens, free or border-holds.[26] Logic would demand that arms could easily be got in the towns and cities of the Free Peoples. METW rules this out, though, and thereby follows Tolkien. The Fellowship of the Ring itself did not acquire many

---

[25] Gollum's home sites are Goblin-gate and Moria and Roäc the Raven can be played at any site in Northern Rhovanion. Saruman's home site is Isengard, which should for all purposes have been made a border-hold.

[26] The exceptions are: Earth of Galadriel's Orchard (playable at Lórien), Ent-draughts (Wellinghall), Palantír of Minas Tirith (Minas Tirith), Red Book of Westmarch (Bag End) and Wizard's Ring (at any haven).

items in Rivendell or in Lórien, but more or less kept the armour and weapons they had found before at different ruins and lairs or obtained from friends. In linking certain items and sites METW successfully adapts many Tolkien features. In the Gladden Fields, for example, only gold rings can be found and the only greater items the Lossadan Cairn offers are palantíri.

Certain places in Middle-earth such as Amon Hen and Dimrill Dale are connected with wisdom and information. At these sites information cards can be played. At the four havens, on the contrary, only very specific information cards can be applied. This is surprising as the havens belonged to the main sources of wisdom and information in Middle-earth.

The havens are prominent, though, when it comes to healing. In addition, healing is also facilitated in Rhosgobel and in the Old Forest, where the positive influence of Radagast and Tom Bombadil is felt.

Mount Doom, finally, is the most special of all sites. No characters, allies, factions, items or information can be brought into the game there. Its sole function is to offer the venue of ending Sauron's threat by destroying the One Ring.

Companies can freely move into havens, free and border-holds, but if they want to enter ruins and lairs, shadow and dark-holds they will have to face automatic attacks.[27] These represent native populations which try to defend their homes against unwelcome intruders. As automatic attacks we often get orcs, but there are also wolves, dragons, trolls, men, spiders, undead and Pûkel-men. Although most automatic attacks make sense – and some like the Ettenmoors with the troll attack are very well chosen indeed – of the 35 sites no less than nine cases are doubtful. The only spider automatic attack, for example, is met at the Ruined Signal Tower in Enedwaith. Shelob, on the contrary, is seldom at home and her lair is guarded by orcs. Another case is the Pûkel-men, who still seem to play a prominent role at the western end of the White Mountains, where they defend the Glittering Caves and the

---

27 The only exception to this rule is Mount Doom, which, despite being a shadow-hold, has not got any automatic attack. As a counter measure it has an increased hazard limit, though.

sites in Andrast and the Old Pûkel Gap. This is, however, not based on literary evidence, as their existence in the western White Mountains of the late Third Age is not documented in Tolkien's works. The gravest deviation concerns the wide spread of undead. They certainly belong to the Barrow-downs, the Dead Marshes, and the Gladden Fields. But there is no evidence at all to have them on Amon Hen or at the leisurely sea-side resorts of Tolfalas. They are even less expected waiting for occasional passers-by on the island of Himring and the Isles of the Dead that Live, the only places in Beleriand which due to their sacred nature were not drowned at the end of the First Age. Who should be haunting the islands? The sons of Fëanor? Or, even worse, Beren and Lúthien?

4 Active Forces

4.1 Characters

The character cards of METW represent the sole independent active forces in the game. Only they can travel round Middle-earth, look out for followers, ask for support from military factions, find allies and search for items that can help them thwart Sauron's plans. The game offers 71 characters, of whom the most important ones are the five wizards Alatar, Gandalf, Pallando, Radagast and Saruman. They are in the centre of action as the companies travelling through Middle-earth do so at their bidding. Of the 66 remaining characters there are fifteen elves, dwarves, Dúnedain and men each and six hobbits[28]. Other species are not represented by characters. Of the 71 characters, no less than 61 are taken directly from Tolkien's writings, although in some cases the characters do not agree with Middle-earth evidence in all their features.

One of the main aims of METW while choosing characters was to represent the peoples and regions as evenly as possible. This was not easy to

---

28 An additional hobbit, Fatty Bolger, was not included in the official set of METW, but offered as a promotional card with the unlimited set of METW.

achieve as the various peoples and regions do not play equally prominent roles in Tolkien's writings. The hobbits posed no problem. The same can be said about the dwarves, who appear plentiful in *The Hobbit* and *The Lord of the Rings*. The elves, however, were more difficult to choose, especially as all elven lands were to be represented. For this reason METW created Annalena and Arinmîr[29] with Edhellond as their home site. The case was most difficult with the mannish cultures. Of the lesser men, ten are taken from Tolkien, whereas five were made up by METW. These characters were largely invented to include peripheral regions in the game. Thus we find a leader of the Lossoth in Vôteli and a Woodmen hero from Mirkwood in Wacho. Other populations that were brought into the game include the Southrons, the Dunlendings and the Men of Dorwinion. Of the fifteen Dúnedain, only eight fit in well with literary evidence. Four characters were taken from Tolkien, but changed to serve the game's purpose, the remaining three are outright inventions by METW. Anborn, Damrod and Mablung are examples of the former. In Tolkien[30] they belong to the Rangers of Ithilien. In METW they are, however, relocated to Lebennin, Lamedon and Anfalas to bring these regions into play. The same happens to Halbarad, who, according to Tolkien, led the Rangers of the North to Rohan. In METW he is turned into the leader of the wild Rhudaur Hillmen. Adrazar, Beretar and Haldalam, on the contrary, are not mentioned in Tolkien's works at all. As their home sites feature alternative characters, their inclusion in the game is not even called for by any necessity. The case is most questionable with Haldalam, who, as a Dúnadan, is found in far-away Dorwinion and is on especially good terms with the Easterlings. The home sites also pose minor problems for two of the wizards, Alatar and Pallando. In Tolkien, the Blue Wizards disappeared into the far east, whereas in METW their home sites are Edhellond and the Grey Havens respectively.[31]

---

29 We get a special surprise with Arinmîr, who is mentioned to be very popular with the Variags, a very unlikely feat for any elf.
30 Tolkien (1981b:333) states that Damrod and Mablung even were of Ithilien descent.
31 J.R.R. Tolkien (1982:392-4). To a lesser degree the same problem also applies to Gimli and Faramir. In the first case, METW chose to remain true to its pre-2941 interpretation

Creating new characters is a tricky business as, like all other characters, they have to get names. This, however, involves once again the danger of awarding these creations the respectability of the genuine. Such a course of action might be tolerable for the game's sake if there are no alternatives, but should be avoided otherwise. It is even more delicate to alter characters. In this case, a character's genuine features are replaced by fake information. This should have been avoided at all costs, even more so as Tolkien offered alternative characters who were not included in the game.

A game like METW can only feature a limited amount of characters and thereby has to omit some which otherwise could be expected. A few of these characters were included as allies. The prime example is Gollum. Some others were introduced later on in METD and MEDM – be it as characters (Galdor, Thrain II, Ioreth, Brand) or as minion agents (Gríma Wormtongue, Bill Ferny). There are, however, also characters which were not included in METW at all. Among them we find a fair number of hobbits, dwarves and prominent Rohirrim lords such as Grimbold of Grimslade, Grimbold of Westfold, Dúnhere of Harrowdale and King Thengel. Further examples of forgotten characters are Erestor from Rivendell, Rúmil from Lórien, Denethor's wife Finduilas, Hirgon from Minas Tirith and Grimbeorn the Old, lord of the Beornings. The alteration of characters, as in the case of Damrod and Mablung, could well have been avoided by adding a few well-chosen characters such as Lord Angbor of Lamedon and Hirluin or Golasgil from Anfalas to the game.

All in all, the choice of characters is highly satisfactory. All major heroes and heroines of the Third Age have been included in METW and Tolkien's creation has undergone but minor additions and alterations. There are even some very interesting characters represented in the game who could not

---

of the Lonely Mountain and therefore put Gimli into the nearest dwarf fortress, i.e. the Iron Hill Dwarf-hold, instead of either the Lonely Mountain or his father's home site, i.e. the Blue Mountain Dwarf-hold. In the second case Henneth Annûn is chosen as Faramir's sole home site, whereas in Tolkien's writings he could as well be found in Minas Tirith.

necessarily have been expected in the game. Among them we find Beregond of the Guards of Minas Tirith, Erkenbrand from Rohan, Beorn, Ghân-buri-Ghân and Robin Smallburrow, the Shirriff.

The distribution of characters, despite all efforts by METW to spread them across the map of Middle-earth, remains highly uneven as no less than 40 out of the 71 characters have as their home site one of the following six: Blue Mountain Dwarf-hold, Bag End, Rivendell, Edoras, Minas Tirith, Lórien. This closely follows the fact, that these sites form the cultural and demographic centres of the Free Peoples. It is also representative of the importance of these Middle-earth areas in the plot development of *The Lord of the Rings* and *The Hobbit*. Eriador as the starting point of the two stories includes the home sites of no less than 34 characters. Wilderland, where the second half of *The Hobbit* and the middle part of *The Lord of the Rings* take place, hosts 22 characters and Gondor, the stage of the final combat in *The Lord of the Rings*, offers home sites to 17 characters. Mordor, on the contrary, as the centre of evil, is the base of none.[32]

In addition to their home sites, characters have a fair number of attributes by which their abilities are defined. The two most important ones are race and skills. Every *race* has certain natural advantages and disadvantages which are represented by a character's additional attributes or by extra cards. In METW each character belongs to one of the following six races: wizard, hobbit, dwarf, elf, Dúnadan and man.

Wizards have numerous spells at their disposal with which they can test rings, weaken attacks on their companies and exert influence. They are, however, exposed to corruption whenever they use such spells. The hobbits' greatest ability is to resist corruption. This ability is manifest in two ways. In the first place they are less often tempted by evil and if they are, they have a natural reluctance to succumb to it. As natural scouts they are better equipped to avoid combat and have an inner strength that far surpasses all

---

32 The addition of these figures does not match the total of characters as Gandalf has all havens as possible home sites.

expectations. Unless they are among the starting characters they cannot be brought into the game outside their beloved Shire and due to their size they only count half towards the size of their companies. Dwarves are the most materialistic of all peoples. Their heirlooms belong to the most powerful items and are especially effective when handled by dwarves. These items, however, easily corrupt their bearers, especially should they be dwarves. They are also natural warriors and have a inborn advantage fighting orcs. While low rank dwarves succumb more easily to temptation and are at a disadvantage exerting influence, this does not apply to high rank dwarves.[33] The elves are the most heterogenous of all races. Among them we find some of the greatest heroes of the Third Age, Elrond, Galadriel and Círdan. The player who controls them can make use of additional options in the game. We also find some special abilities with Arwen and Celeborn, who exert a strong influence on their spouses. The remaining elves have varying attributes. Some of them have combat advantages against orcs, while others exert influence over certain characters or factions with either more or less ease than usual. In general, elves are stronger both physically and mentally and show more skills than comparable characters. They are, however, more susceptible to mental weariness. The Dúnedain's great advantage lies in bringing Dúnedain and men factions into play. In addition they are natural warriors and have healing faculties the other races do not have. The lesser men retain the same advantage bringing men factions into play, but have more varied attributes than the Dúnedain. An additional highly important ability is found in female mannish characters, who have a huge combat advantage against Nazgûls.[34]

---

33 Not even to Thorin II who in the original story was corrupted by greed in the Quest of Erebor.

34 This is based on Glorfindel's prophecy regarding the fate of the Witch-king of Angmar as found in Tolkien (1981c:407). The original prophecy has, however, been altered in two important aspects. In *The Lord of the Rings*, the prophecy referred only to the Witch-king, whereas in METW this has been extended to mean all Nazgûls. At the same time the threat has been reduced from all non-men to female characters of lower mannish descent.

The second highly important personal attribute in METW is *skill*. Whereas a character can only be of one race, he may have several skills. Therefore the skills are more widely spread over the characters. The characters can have one or more of the five following skills: warrior, scout, ranger, sage, diplomat.

The most basic and at the same time most obvious skill in METW is the warrior skill, which is directly linked to combat and leadership abilities. No less than 50 out of 71 characters are warriors. Although the best fighters are all warriors, there are some warriors who are physically inferior to a number of non-warriors. Warriors are, however, able to improve their offensive and defensive fighting abilities by using special weapons or fighting techniques and may muster military factions more easily. The second most common skill is the scout skill which is found with 28 characters. The scouts' main ability lies in keeping small companies out of danger and finding hidden treasures. We find a similar skill in the ranger skill, which is found with 21 characters. They are the greatest nature experts. They are the only ones who may lead companies over high mountain ranges, across broad rivers or through adverse ecological and weather conditions. The sage skill, which is limited to 20 characters, enables its bearer to gain and use highly specialized knowledge, make use of magical objects such as palantíri and test rings. 22 characters have the diplomat skill, which helps them bring in new factions and keep fellow company members from joining other companies or from falling to the dark side.

The playing options which are linked to race and skills fit in very well with Middle-earth evidence. The same can be said of most characters' endowment with skills. There are, however, a few exceptions to this rule. One major problem lies in those characters who do not play clearly defined parts in Tolkien's stories, but had to be given skills for the game's sake. A prime example of this is Barliman Butterbur. In METW he is given the warrior skill, although no Middle-earth evidence can be found for it. The only skill that could possibly be imagined for an inn-keeper like him would be the diplomat skill. Similar cases we find in Bergil, who makes a good scout but certainly not a warrior, and also in Arwen. Her sage skill is well chosen, but in addition to that she would have made a much better diplomat than a scout. Also no evidence is found for Halbarad's skills. In *The Lord of the Rings* he looks much more the average warrior and ranger Dúnadan than a sage and diplomat. Surprising skills were, however, also attributed to some major characters such as Elrond, Galadriel and Círdan. Whereas their sage and diplomat skills are in no doubt, their qualities as warriors and scouts do not go down well. We get the same problem with Sam Gamgee who makes a good scout, but hardly a good ranger.

The characters' physical qualities are given in two separate measurements. The first one is called *prowess* and describes a character's offensive capabilities in combat. The second one, *body*, represents a character's ability of surviving injuries.[35]

In METW top rates for both prowess and body go to the elven lords, the wizards and some selected mannish heroes such as Beorn and Aragorn. Boromir, on the contrary, has also got a top prowess rate, but only second-rate body. The dwarves are found in mid-field on both scales, whereas the Hobbits combine bottom prowess with top body rates. Among the Rohirrim, finally, prowess improves with age, but the opposite applies to the body rates. The METW ratings agree with Middle-earth evidence in a large number of cases. General disagreement can, however, be found in the case of the elven lords, whose top prowess rates stand in stark contrast with their lack of fighting practice, and in the case of the dwarves, whose mediocre body rates badly render their hardiness. Among the Rohirrim there is also a bias against youth as in the cases of Éomer and Éowyn, who get prowess and body rates notably lower than what would be expected from *The Lord of the Rings*. Boromir's low body rate seems to be in accordance with his premature death, but hardly takes its circumstances into consideration. A last problem we get with the elven ladies. Whereas Galadriel's high body

---

35 ICE (1996:17).

suits her fine, her prowess and both Arwen's prowess and body rates are clearly set too high.

The characters' mental qualities are assessed by two criteria called *direct influence* and *mind*. The first one represents the leadership qualities and personal authority, which are needed to influence other characters and win the support of military factions. The second one is a sign for a character's mental strength and determines how many influence points are required to control him.

The wizards are the only characters who have enough direct influence to form substantial companies under their personal leadership. As they have no specific mind points, they cannot be controlled by other characters. Apart from them, it is again the elven lords who have the highest direct influence and mind points, closely followed by mannish and dwarfen lords. The midfield is filled with middle-rank heroes and local chieftains, whereas a large number of characters have only got few mind points and zero direct influence. The most important factors for direct influence points are office and age, while some racial preference can also be found in the case of the hobbits. The mind points, on the other hand, may also take strength of character into account, as is the case with Thorin Oakenshield's high mind points.[36] The game's direct influence and mind point ratings fit in well with Middle-earth evidence with the exception of the hobbits, who get too high ratings. It is very unlikely that a halfling could demand more obedience than a young Rohirrim prince such as Éomer.

The characters have another two personal attributes, the *corruption check modifier* and the *marshalling points*. The first one represents a character's innate ability to resist the temptation of falling to the dark side. The marshalling points, on the contrary, stand for his importance to the Free People's struggle against Sauron. They show the prestige the character is

---

36 This is, however, not always the case as Denethor and Boromir only get relatively low mind points.

lending his wizard at the Free Council and are directly linked to his mind points. To this effect the marshalling points belong to the most strategically important features of the characters.

4.2 Companies

The characters can travel round Middle-earth and take various actions all on their own. This, however, means that they have to face the hazards they are going to meet on their own, too. This is a highly risky strategy. In order to avoid this, characters can form companies thereby also reducing the number of dangerous hazards they may meet on their way. The basic advantage of forming companies, however, consists in the option of having stronger characters protect weaker ones. A second advantage lies in the possibility of supporting each other morally if one of them is tempted to join another wizard or to fall to the dark side. The size of the companies is best decided by the strategies the players want to adopt. Small companies are useful if they want to make use of certain allies who allow movement by stealth or speed. Large companies, on the other hand, are better in combat and preferable if huge objects such as certain palantíri are to be acquired and moved around Middle-earth. Working as companies rather than as individuals is an important feature of both *The Lord of the Rings* and *The Hobbit*. The encouragement of forming companies, therefore, must be seen as a great asset to METW.

4.3 Allies

There are a number of important characters in Tolkien's books, who cannot be subsumed under the races mentioned above. As METW wanted to include them in the game but not as characters, a separate category had to be created for them. As a sub-category of the resource cards, the allies cannot act independently, but support the characters that have brought them into play. An ally is, however, not a simple resource to be used like an item, but has character attributes such as skills, mind, prowess, body, marshalling points as well as some special abilities all of which enable him to take a limited amount of actions.

We find four Ents (Leaflock, Quickbeam, Skinbark, Treebeard), Tom Bombadil and his spouse Goldberry, Gollum and four animals (Shadowfax, Bill the Pony, Gwaihir and Roäc the Raven) among the allies. All of them played important parts in *The Lord of the Rings* or in *The Hobbit* and no further allies suggest themselves from Tolkien's works. Their inclusion as allies with limited freedom of action (and of movement, in some cases) rather than as free and independent characters fits in well with literary evidence in all but one case. Endowed with a free and intelligent spirit, Gollum has no limits of fully cooperating with other characters, even if it is to his own ends rather than any wizard's. He should much rather have been included in METW as a character than as an ally.

5 Chances and Dangers

The various companies are travelling through Middle-earth in order to gain the resources that may help them defeat Sauron or to make the wizard they are following the leader of the Free Council. Among the most important furnishers of the marshalling points which are needed to achieve the second aim the members of the companies themselves are found. In addition, marshalling points can also be gained by securing the support of military factions, by acquiring various items or by carrying out certain actions. All these activities are, however, not free from danger. A great amount of highly varying hazards can beset the companies, among them attacks by Sauron's followers, local resistance, adverse ecological and weather conditions and various forms of temptation. The METW features which enable a player to win the game are represented by character and resource cards, whereas the dangers take the form of hazard cards.

5.1 Factions

One of the ways of winning the prestige necessary to be elected leader of the Free Council is by gaining the support of military factions. In order to achieve this, companies have to travel to the home sites of the factions and ask for their support. The factions, however, do not pledge their support to anybody asking for it, but are free to give it or to withhold it. This element of arbitrariness is represented by a roll of dice. Its result is, however, modified by such factors as the race and skills of the character undertaking the influence bid, his personal prestige and his standing with the faction concerned.

In METW there are no less than 29 factions. Two of them each are made up of dwarves, elves and Drúedain, four of them are Dúnedain factions and fifteen are of lower mannish descent. In addition, we also find one faction each of hobbits, ents and eagles and the famous Army of the Dead. There is a very high representation of lower mannish populations[37], which owes much to the fact that the other cultures only play relatively minor parts in the racial composition of Third Age Middle-earth. Of the 29 factions there are only four whose availability is doubtful. For one there is no evidence of the existence of Drúedain in late Third Age Old Pûkel-land in Tolkien's writings and furthermore the Easterlings, Southrons and Variags of Khand are very unlikely supporters of the Free Peoples.[38] The inclusion of the Army of the Dead, on the contrary, belongs to the highlights of the game.

Military factions do not play any active part in the game, but remain idle in the background. METW puts a great amount of emphasis on single actions by companies of limited size, which fits in well with Middle-earth evidence. Large parts of *The Lord of the Rings* and *The Hobbit* deal with such actions, including the key scene of the destruction of the One Ring on Mount Doom. The actions of huge military factions such as the defence of

---

37 This is enforced by the fact that only three of the Gondorean factions are of Dúnedain descent and four of lower mannish descent.

38 The Easterlings, Southrons and Variags would have made much better supporters of Sauron, i.e. hazard creatures. METW could have replaced them by the elvish factions from Rivendell and Lórien or by the mannish factions from Bree, Andrast and Tolfalas.

the Hornburg, the Ride of the Rohirrim and the taking of the corsair ships by the Army of the Dead should, however, not be underestimated either. The game could have been improved by rendering actions by military factions possible. This, however, has been ruled out by METW.

5.2 Items

Items belong to the most powerful resource cards in METW. On the one hand, most of them carry marshalling points, which are important for players who go for the Free Council-option. On the other hand, they also lend additional abilities and opportunities to the characters controlling them. Their only blemish, however, lies in the corruption points they burden the characters with.

As could be expected, rings are one of the most important kinds of items. They are, however, also the most difficult ones to bring into play, as they require a two-tier approach, should they be put to full use. The first action consists of finding a gold ring at one of the sites where gold rings can be played.[39] The ring at this point is of no great use, though, as the person carrying it does not know its identity and abilities yet. For this reason, the ring must be tested. Of the four kinds of rings mentioned in *The Lord of the Rings*, only the One Ring and the seven dwarven rings are playable in METW. The elven rings, on the contrary, are given to Galadriel, Elrond and Gandalf, who may reveal them in need[40], and the nine rings of men, finally, do not enter the game as they are connected with the Nazgûls. In addition, however, the ring can also be turned into one of five different magic rings (each of them linked to one of the five skills) or a lesser ring. Most powerful of all is the One Ring, which offers its bearer huge additional direct

---

39 Gold rings can only be found on the Gladden Fields, at Goblin-gate, Ost-in-Edhil, Moria, Isengard, at the Bandit Lair, on the Isles of the Dead that Live and at the four dragon lairs.

40 To limit the use of the elven rings and bring it into the right perspective with their use in Middle-earth, METW has included them as short-events rather than items. In this form, they can only be used when they come up during the game.

influence, prowess and body, but also burdens him with huge additional corruption. Carrying the One Ring makes the bearer much stronger, but also exposes him to constant high levels of temptation. Next in line are the seven dwarven rings, which similarly influence their bearers (especially should they be dwarves), but also reflect their old masters' desires by enabling dwarves to track down items rather than come across them. The magic rings, on the other hand, give the bearers the extra skill they are linked to or enhance it if the bearer has already got it. The Wizard's Ring can only be played on a wizard and improves his direct influence, prowess and body, while burdening him with high additional corruption. The lesser rings, finally, add to the bearer's direct influence. The mechanics of ring testing and the corruption connected with the rings add a lot to the Middle-earth quality of the game.

Another important aspect of Tolkien, which was included in METW, is the use of palantíri. The game features the seeing-stones of the White Towers, Orthanc and Minas Tirith, which can only be found at their home sites, as well as the ones of Amon Sûl, Annúminas and Osgiliath, whose whereabouts are to be discovered. The palantír of Minas Ithil, on the contrary, was lost to Sauron and cannot be used in METW. The different palantíri offer the bearers different advantages, most of which have to do with looking into the future or finding out the opponent's aims. Like in Tolkien's works the palantíri are seldom used and if so, at high risk, but they can also be of great help.

Weapons and armour also belong to the most useful items in METW. We find some of the most renowned weapons and pieces of armour of Middle-earth (Orcrist, Glamdring, Narsil, Durin's Axe, Sting, the mithril-coat), but also some general items. The weapons generally have a positive influence on prowess, while the pieces of armour improve the body rates. Some weapons also have additional bonuses depending on who wields the weapon or against whom it is wielded. A very special feature is found with Narsil, which can be reforged into Andúril.

METW offers a great amount of additional items. Some of them belong to the most important items of Third Age history (Book of Mazarbul, Scroll of Isildur, Arkenstone, Red Arrow), whereas others are only of local interest (Earth of Galadriel's Orchard, Red Book of Westmarch) or of everyday usage (athelas, healing herbs, miruvor, etc.). With one exception all of these items are taken from Tolkien's books and their special abilities generally agree well with Middle-earth evidence.

The quantity of items in METW and their variety add a great deal to the interest of the game as well as to its overall quality as a representation of Tolkien's world. The same can be said of the single items, which, with the exception of a very few cases, are true to Tolkien's creation.

5.3 Resource Events

The companies are mainly interested in acquiring ever more resources that may be of help in their struggle against Sauron. On their travels, however, they constantly meet danger in various forms. In order to survive, they need all the help they can get. This help often is represented by resource events.

A large amount of resource events are used to realize the positive influence of company-building and the various abilities of the different skills and races. A second group of events helps the companies to overcome or to avoid attacks by modifiying their respective strengths, limiting their numbers or even cancelling them due to some positive environmental influence. A third group of events enables companies to move faster or further than they normally do.

Apart from these common uses, there are also some major Middle-earth features which have been translated into resource events. Aragorn, for example, can take the Paths of the Dead to the Stone of Erech in order to marshall the Army of the Dead and once in Minas Tirith he can profit from his very own Return of the King if Denethor is not in play. Both actions leave him with high marshalling points. Further features that have been included in METW include the White Tree, the Mirror of Galadriel, Gollum's Fate on Mount Doom, the Sacrifice of Form (Gandalf's physical death and resurrection), the Secret Entrance (Moria's West-door) and the

Eagle-mounts (eagle-transport as found in *The Hobbit*). Even the use of the elven rings is regulated in the form of resource events. The inclusion of these Middle-earth features highly contributes to the quality of the game as a representation of Tolkien's works.

5.4 Hazard Creatures

Hazard creatures are by far the most dangerous and most direct threat to the characters in play. Their aim is to attack anybody they are coming across. As a rule they are restricted to specified regions or sites or, as an alternative, to the regions or the sites of a certain type. If they succeed in their attacks, their victims most often are wounded or even killed, although there are some hazard creatures who take a victim's belongings rather than his life. If, on the contrary, a company can defeat a creature, it gets a reward in the form of marshalling points. The amount of marshalling points varies between the creatures, as it is related to the creature's ferocity and importance, and represents the prestige that a successful defence lends to a company.

The most terrible of all hazard creatures are, of course, the nine Nazgûls. They are almost indestructable, unless the company contains a woman of lesser mannish descent. Their centre lies in Mordor, with major outposts in Dol Guldur and Angmar and they constantly patrol the regions linking these core areas of evil. As each of their rounds covers different parts of the patrol area, though, every one of them has a very limited range of action. In order to attack companies on a broad basis, they need additional means of transport or more favourable environmental conditions. In Tolkien's works only two Nazgûls are mentioned by name, the Witch-king of Angmar and Khamûl the Easterling. As METW decided to include all nine Nazgûls as individual hazard creatures, the remaining seven had to be given invented names. Although this technique is far from ideal, it cannot be avoided, should the atmosphere of Middle-earth be transformed into the game.

We face a similar problem with the dragons as no less than three out of the four individual dragons of METW got names invented by the gamemakers. The dragons are only fractionally weaker than Nazgûls, but their range of action is far smaller. Under normal circumstances it is limited to the dragon's home site, although under certain conditions they can cover the four regions of the Iron Hills, the Grey Mountain Narrows, the Withered Heath and Northern Rhovanion or attack at a number of ruins and lairs.

All other individual hazard creatures were taken from Tolkien's works with the exception of a troll called Rogrog. Among the remaining individuals, we find some of the most important dark heroes such as the three stone-trolls and the Great Goblin from *The Hobbit* and Shelob, the Silent Watcher, the Watcher in the Water and the Mouth of Sauron from *The Lord of the Rings*. The biggest number of hazard creatures, however, are defined by their occupation, their race or their species. Among them we find assassins, ambushers, thieves, giants, giant spiders and various factions of orcs, trolls and animals. The choice of hazard creatures is very good and the game acquires a distinctive Tolkien flavour by including a high number of unique creatures such as corpse-candles, barrow-wights, crebain, huorns, wargs, the Old Man Willow and also the corsairs of Umbar. There are, however, two cases, which are less fortunate. First there are the Pûkel-men, who do not only defend their natural habitat, but according to METW are also found at the various shadow and dark-holds and secondly the ghouls, who are out of place in a game based on Tolkien. They can be included in any one of the hundred other role playing and collectable card games.

5.5 Hazard Events

The hazard events generally aim at rendering the environment hostile to the companies of the Free Peoples. A large amount of them does so by mirroring corresponding resource events. Therefore we find a number of events which improve the combat chances of hazard creatures and automatic attacks by modifying their strengths and enlarging their numbers and their range of action. A second group of events represents Sauron's negative influence on the environment. These events mainly work by applying new region types to certain regions thereby opening them to new kinds of attacks. A further group of environmental events represents the hazards of nature itself. They hinder movement rather than constitute a real threat to the companies as they force them to go back to their sites of origin or to remain idle at their new sites. The former can also be achieved by sieges.

There is a further group of events, though, which is of prime importance to the game. It consists of events which have an influence on the corruption of characters. Some of them increase a character's innate corruptibility, whereas others lead characters into temptation. The most terrible examples of such events are found in connection with wounds made by Nazgûl weapons. Homesickness and the elves' longing for the sea form similar, if less powerful, phenomena as the characters are not overwhelmed by corruption, but only feel the very strong urge to leave their companies. The same can happen to military factions which feel tempted to sever their alliances.

METW also includes a fair amount of hazard events by which important Middle-earth features such as the corrupting influence of rings can be realized. Similarly, Nazgûls have a highly limited range of movement, that can be extended only be special means such as Morgul-horses and Fell Beasts or by special environmental events such as Morgul Night. Further examples of successful adaptations of Middle-earth features include the Balrog of Moria, the Bane of the Ithil-stone (corrupting influence of palantíri), Traitor (Gríma Wormtongue's treason), the Burden of Time (elves' weariness of life), the Despair of the Heart (Denethor's despair at losing his son) and the Call of Home (Sam's homesickness). These features heighten the Middle-earth atmosphere of METW and highly contribute to the quality of the game as a representation of Tolkien's works.

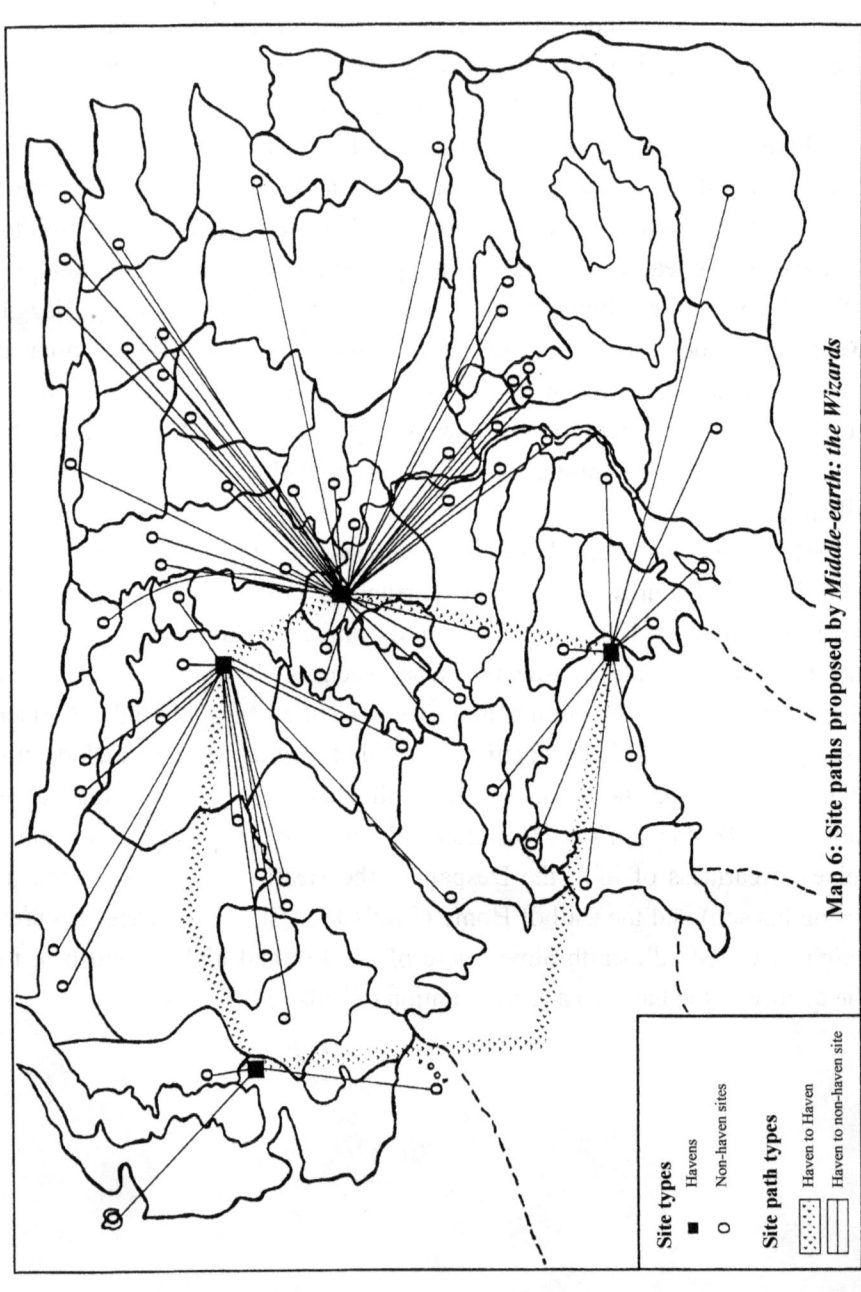

Map 6: Site paths proposed by *Middle-earth: the Wizards*

6 Movement

METW offers the companies two parallel types of movement. The first one relies on the schematic site paths printed on the site cards and is therefore called site path movement. The second one relies on the specific regions the companies are moving through and is therefore called region movement.

Site path movement is comparable to today's airport hub system. A company cannot go wherever it wants, but has to move to a site which is linked with the original site by its site path (as reproduced in Map 6). For havens this means one of the two nearest fellow-havens or one of the non-haven sites listing it as its nearest haven. For a non-haven site, on the contrary, there is only one site to go to: its nearest haven. A company at Lórien, for example, may move to Rivendell, Edhellond (its two nearest havens) or to any one of the 36 non-haven sites listing it as its nearest haven. A company in Rhosgobel, on the contrary, can only go to Lórien.

Under the rules of site path movement, the travel from a haven (Lórien) to a neighbouring haven or to any one of its connected non-haven sites (Wellinghall, Iron Hill Dwarf-hold) takes one turn of play regardless of the distance covered. At the same time, the movement between two non-heaven sites linked with the same heaven (Rhosgobel and Beorn's House) invariably takes two turns and the travel between two sites, which are not linked to the same haven (Isengard and Dunnish Clan-hold), takes three or four turns. The time a journey takes by site path movement is only related to the amount of site paths connecting the two sites, not, however, to the distance lying between the two sites.

Region movement, on the contrary, does not take site paths into consideration. It allows a company to travel from any one site to any other site provided that they lie no more than four regions apart (original and destination region included). As a result, short-distance travels from Rhosgobel to Beorn's House or from Isengard to the Dunnish Clan-hold take only one turn of play, whereas long-distance travels such as from Lórien to the Iron Hill dwarf-hold take two. The time travel takes by region movement is only linked to the number of regions lying between two sites and the obstacles found on the way, thereby laying a regular pattern of movement over the map of Middle-earth.

The two movement systems also lead to two differing hazard patterns. Site path movement does not lead a company through specific regions, but through certain region types. As a result only creatures keyed to the region types can be played on the company, not, however, creatures keyed to the specific regions. This is not the case with region movement, which allows creatures both keyed to specific regions and region types to be played on the company.

If, for example, a company moves from Lórien to the Easterling Camp by site path movement, the company does not travel through the regions of Wold & Foothills, Brown Lands, Dagorlad and Horse Plains, but through one wilderness and three shadow-lands. The hazards that can be played against the company therefore are not hazards keyed to Wold & Foothills, Brown Lands, Dagorlad and Horse Plains, but hazards keyed to the wilderness and shadow-land region types. By region movement, however, both creatures keyed to the above-mentioned region types and to the individual regions can be played. This means, that when using site path movement, the company cannot be attacked by any Nazgûls. However, if it uses region movement, it must prepare for Khamûl the Easterling and five other Nazgûls.

The movement rules of METW allow the simultaneous use of both site path and region movement. This, however, results in highly differing movement and hazard patterns. As site path movement leads to most bizarre travel routes[41], its inclusion in METW as a movement type of equal value must be

---

41 The movement from Rhosgobel to neighbouring Beorn's House, for example, can only be done via Lórien under the rules of site path movement.

seen as a major flaw of the game. The sole use of region movement is the only option which can be justified by Middle-earth evidence.[42]

7 Influence

Influence is an important feature of METW. It is generally used to exert control over characters and allies and to muster military factions. It is realized in two versions. The first one, general influence, is attributed to the wizards and represents their innate power as emissaries from Aman. The second one, direct influence, is given to a selected group of characters (including the wizards) and is linked to their personal prestige. A character can improve his direct influence by acquiring certain important items, but there are also some resource events which temporarily add to his prestige and personal direct influence. In addition, some characters have positive direct influence modifiers towards individual characters and factions due to their personal relations and kinship. Other characters, however, have general negative direct influence modifiers due to their low standing in society.[43] The military factions themselves can have direct influence modifiers, too, which respond to the race of the character who makes an influence attempt. If the character is of a race for which the faction mentions a positive modification, then it is easier for him to muster the faction. If there is a

---

42 There remains a major problem with the drawing of cards, though. In METW both the active player and his opponent draw a number of random cards determined by the site they are moving to (or the site they are moving from, if the new destination is a haven). The number of cards they draw is related to the chances and dangers connected with the individual site and its site path. If, however, site path movement is rejected as a type of movement, the number of cards to be drawn must be doubted, too, as the chances and dangers met on the way from the nearest haven to the site need not necessarily be the same as the ones met on the way from somewhere else. The number of cards to be drawn should, therefore, much rather depend on the site type of the destination and the region types of the regions the company travels through. The game, however, does not offer any alternative card-drawing mechanism based on region and site types.

43 This is, for example, the case with all lower class dwarves. As dwarves are not that popular with the other Free Peoples and lower class dwarves do not have any prestige within dwarven society, their general negative direct influence modifiers are well justified by Middle-earth evidence.

negative modifier for his race, the influence attempt is made more difficult. The only character who can have an effect on the influence attempt is the influencing character himself. The racial composition of his company, on the contrary, does not affect the attempt. There is no difference to the outcome of the influence attempt on a dwarvish military faction, whether the influencing dwarf's company consists of six dwarves or of one dwarf and five elves. Middle-earth evidence, however, points to strong racial likes and dislikes, which should not be seen limited to the influencing character, but also extended to the fellow company members.

Most influence attempts are made on characters, allies and factions which are not in play yet. In this case the influencing character tries to persuade the target of the attempt that it is in the common interest to join forces. Influence attempts of this kind are straightforward, as they only involve a comparison of the influencing character's direct influence and the target's mind points and a single roll of dice. Influence attemps can, however, also be made on characters, allies and factions which are already in play. In that case the influencing character tries to convince the target of the attempt that it is in the common interest that he breaks off the present alliance and either goes his own way or even joins forces with the influencing character's company. This second kind of influence attempt can also be made on items. In that case the influencing character tries to persuade his opponent to give up a certain item as it is more effective in his hands. An influence attempt of the second kind always represents a power struggle between the two sides involved and therefore must take the influence of both sides into account. A roll of dice by both players as well as a comparison of various forms of influence points decides on the outcome of the influence attempt. The mechanism sorting out influence attempts is rather complicated, but serves its purpose well with one exception. If the influencing player can reveal a card which is identical to the target's, there is no numerical advantage to be found for either of the two sides. This, however, clearly contradicts Middle-earth evidence, as companionship and loyalty are high moral values in

Tolkien's writings. A numerical advantage to the present controlling character should be set on principal.

8 Corruption

One of the most interesting features of METW is corruption. It is largely unknown to other collectable card games. Going through adventures, risking one's own life, finding valuable and powerful items and gaining influence over other people can tempt even the strongest characters to forget the common good and the quest they set out to fulfil. Corruption is one of the central, if not the most important subject of *The Lord of the Rings*, a work which can be summed up by the catch-phrase "Power corrupts and total power corrupts totally". In this spirit Boromir tried to take the One Ring from Frodo to save Gondor from Sauron's onslaught and to win fame as the greatest warlord of his time. Similarly Saruman was corrupted into believing that he could use its power to control the world in a manner he himself saw as desirable. Galadriel also felt the power of the ring, but like Gandalf, was strong enough to resist it. Frodo, finally, fought the ring all the way to Mount Doom just to succumb to its wooing at the very end. Corruption, however, also worked in small portions as is witnessed by Sam's temptation to leave the Fellowship of the Ring, when he saw the ruin of the Shire in Galadriel's Mirror. Even positive feelings like a person's love for his home may corrupt and undo all he is fighting for. Corruption as one of Tolkien's most important topics should not be absent in any Tolkien-related game and the high quality of its realization in METW makes corruption one of the greatest assets of the game.

In METW corruption does not affect all characters the same way. The hobbits have a natural reluctance to succumb to it, whereas the dwarves as the most materialistic of all races are the most obvious targets. Moreover, the acquisition and use of powerful items expose the characters to the temptation which is linked to the chances the items offer. In a similar manner the wizards are affected by the use of spells. Almost all items which may be of some use to their owners as well as most actions which may have a favourable effect on the persons carrying them out expose the characters to further corruption. Under certain conditions, the characters will then have to undergo corruption checks. If a character fails one of his corruption checks, he will lose his belief in the common cause and betray his fellow companions. In grave cases, he may even be lost to the cause of the Free Peoples for ever.

Corruption plays a highly important part in METW. This is in perfect agreement with literary evidence, as corruption was one of the prime agents in *The Lord of the Rings*. In both the game and its literary source, it belongs to the most dangerous hazard conditions characters can face and is one of the most common causes of their undoing.

III. CONCLUSION

Apart from its quality as a game, *Middle-earth: the Wizards* is highly successful as a representation of late Third Age Middle-earth as described in *The Lord of the Rings* and *The Hobbit*. The general atmosphere of the period is well translated into the game and its many details are most pleasing to the Tolkien enthusiast. Iron Crown Enterprises, the producer of the game, put considerable care into maintaining the spirit of Tolkien's works and, in its publication, *Middle-earth: the Wizards Companion*, made sure to point the reader (and player) to the ultimate source of information on Middle-earth, J.R.R. Tolkien's books. All major characters, items and events of the late Third Age have been included as playing cards and the distinctive features of Tolkien's works are represented both in the cards and the rules of the game. Furthermore, its treatment of corruption and its analysis of Middle-earth geography are great assets to the game. The Tolkien purist may wince at the rather extensive invention and alteration of characters and sites. For the most part, however, these distortions were necessitated by the requirements of the *genus* game or the need of filling gaps of information in Tolkien's creation. These alterations and additions, unfortunate as they may be, very rarely clash with the primary sources and their omission would have left the game unworkable and, surprisingly enough, with a reduced Tolkien flavour. There are also some major methodological flaws such as the messed up time-scheme and the coexistence of two conflicting movement systems. The players should, however, feel free to develop alternative sets of rules whenever they feel the official rules of the game to be in conflict with Middle-earth evidence.

There have also been two thematic expansion sets to *Middle-earth: the Wizards*, namely *Middle-earth: the Dragons* and *Middle-earth: the Dark Minions*.[44] While, on the one hand, they develop the main motives of the basic set further, they also introduce new resource and hazard strategies such as hoard-hunting, dragons and covert action by minion agents. The expansion sets, however, face one big problem. Much of what we know about the Third Age of Middle-earth, has already been released in the basic set, which in itself had to resort to the invention of new material in order to fill some of the gaps left by J. R. R. Tolkien. This problem is much worse for the expansion sets. They had to include large amounts of non-authentic material to make their new game features work. Only a small minority of the new sites, dragon hazard creatures and minion agents are taken from Tolkien's works. Most of them, on the contrary, were invented by the game makers. While some of the new game features are attractive in themselves, the expansion sets show the absolute limits to which the qualitative boundaries can be stretched. Further developments of the *Middle-earth Collectable Card Game* are only conceivable in the new field Iron Crown Entreprises has recently opened with *Middle-earth: The Lidless Eye*, i.e. the dark side of the same conflict. In it, the nine Nazgûls compete for Sauron's preference by looking for the One Ring and mustering as many resources as possible.

---

44 This was true at the time of the writing of this article, as there were to be four more expansion sets later on.

It would be much more interesting, however, to work out an entirely new game based on the events of the Elder Days. Why not *Middle-earth: the Silmarils* in which the Sons of Fëanor, Elu Thingol and the Naugrim of Nogrod all fight for the possession of the Silmarils? There is so much interesting material asking for representation in that age. In the mean-time, we can only bide our time and enjoy the pleasure *Middle-earth: the Wizard* is offering us.

References

FONSTAD, Karen Wynn. 1992. *The Atlas of Middle-Earth*. 2nd revised edition. First edition 1981. Reprinted as paperback 1994. London: HarperCollins.

ICE (publishers). 1995. *Middle-earth: the Wizards. Rulesbook*. Charlottesville, Virginia: Iron Crown Enterprises.

– – –. 1996. *Middle-earth: the Wizards Companion*. Charlottesville, Virginia: Iron Crown Enterprises.

NÄF, PATRICK. 2004. »Middle-earth: The Collectible Card Game – Powerplay in the World of Tolkien« In: Peter Buchs and Thomas Honegger (eds.). 2004. *News from the Shire and Beyond. Studies on Tolkien*. 2nd revised edition. Zurich and Berne: Walking Tree Publishers, 83-102.

TOLKIEN, J.R.R. 1981a. *The Fellowship of the Ring*. Unwin Paperbacks. London: Allen and Unwin.

– – –. 1981b. *The Two Towers*. Unwin Paperbacks. London: Allen and Unwin.

– – –. 1981c. *The Return of the King*. Unwin Paperbacks. London: Allen and Unwin.

– – –. 1981d. *The Hobbit*. Unwin Paperbacks. London: Allen and Unwin.

– – –. 1982. *Unfinished Tales of Númenor and Middle-earth*. Ed. by Christopher Tolkien. Unwin Paperbacks. London: Allen and Unwin.

TYLER, J.E.A. 1979. *The New Tolkien Companion*. Picador. London: Pan Books.

NOTES ON THE CONTRIBUTORS

Peter Buchs read History and English Linguistics & Literature at the University of Zurich. His 'Lizentiatsarbeit' (M.A. thesis) was on *The Singular Pronouns of Address in English Dialects of the 20th Century*. He is currently working for the Swiss Statistical Office being responsible for the Swiss Entreprise Census. He was one of the founding members of the Swiss Tolkien Society and has served as its chairman from 1986 to 1998 and as the editor of its magazine, *Aglared*, from 1986 to 1993. He has taken active part in literary conferences on Tolkien at The Hague 1990, Delft 1996 and at Seelisberg 1996, where he was a co-organiser, in Brielle 2001 and Balmberg 2001. Peter is married and a father of two, a son born in 1997 and a daughter born in 1999.

Thomas Honegger holds a Ph.D. from the University of Zurich where he had been working as assistant and where he taught Old and Middle English. He is the author of *From Phoenix to Chauntecleer: Medieval English Animal Poetry* (1996) and has edited *News from the Shire and Beyond – Studies on Tolkien* (1997, together with Peter Buchs), *Root and Branch – Approaches towards Understanding Tolkien* (1999), *Authors, Heroes and Lovers* (2001), *Tolkien in Translation* (2003) and *Riddles, Knights and Cross-Dressing Saints* (2004). Apart from his publications on animals and Tolkien, he has written about Chaucer, Shakespeare, and medieval romance. His 'Habilitationsschrift' focused on the interaction between lovers in medieval narrative fiction. He is, since April 2002, Professor for Medieval Studies at the Friedrich-Schiller-University (Jena) and currently head of the department.

Nils-Lennart Johannesson was educated at Stockholm University and Yale University. He received his Ph.D. from Stockholm University in 1976. He worked as Junior Research Fellow and Associate Professor at the English Department, Stockholm University, for thirteen years before becoming Professor of English Language at the English Department, University of Trondheim, in 1991. In 2000 he transferred to the English Language Chair at the University of Stockholm, Sweden. His publications (in addition to articles on Tolkien's languages and Old and Middle English) include *The Dress of Thought: Aspects of the Study of Language* (ed., 1986), *English Language Essays: Investigation Method and Writing Strategies* (4th ed., 1993), *Nonstandard Varieties of Language* (ed. with G. Melchers, 1994). He is currently working on a new edition of the *Ormulum*, a 12th century homily collection.

Patrick Näf is currently employed as a software engineer by a Switzerland based, international manufacturer and supplier of medical devices such as electrocardiographs and spirometers. His passion for games of all types is only surpassed by his intense relationship with books, among which he most avidly reads stories of Science Fiction and Fantasy. Ever since his teen-age encounter with *The Hobbit*, a part of him has been lost to Tolkien's wonderful creation of Middle-earth. In this world, he lives with his partner near Lucerne in central Switzerland.

The Swiss Tolkien Society 'EREDAIN'

The Swiss Tolkien Society 'EREDAIN' was founded in 1986. Our main aims are to further the study of and the interest in the life and work of late Prof. J.R.R. Tolkien and contribute to the enjoyment of his creation, Middle-earth, in Switzerland. Our society organises Tolkien-related events such as quizzes and public readings, rejoices in outdoor activities ('down the Anduin' and 'through the mines of Moria') and edits a fanzine named 'Aglared' on a yearly basis. The members of 'EREDAIN' share the pleasure in Tolkien's creation with our sister societies in many countries near and far.

If you are interested in our activities, please visit our website at www.eredain.ch or contact us via:

kontakt@eredain.ch

or

Swiss Tolkien Society
P.O. Box 1916
CH-8021 Zurich
Switzerland

Walking Tree Publishers was founded in 1997 as a forum for publications of material (books, videos, CDs, etc.) related to Tolkien and Middle-earth studies. Manuscripts and project proposals can be submitted to the board of editors (please include an SAE):

Walking Tree Publishers
CH-3052 Zollikofen
Switzerland
e-mail: walkingtree@go.to
http://go.to/walkingtree

Publications:

Cormarë Series

News from the Shire and Beyond. Studies on Tolkien.
> Edited by Peter Buchs and Thomas Honegger. Zurich and Berne 2004. Reprint. 1st edition 1997. (Cormarë Series 1)

Root and Branch. Approaches towards Understanding Tolkien.
> Edited by Thomas Honegger. Zurich and Berne 2004. Reprint. 1st edition 1999. (Cormarë Series 2)

Richard Sturch. *Four Christian Fantasists. A Study of the Fantastic Writings of George MacDonald, Charles Williams, C. S. Lewis and J.R.R. Tolkien.* Zurich and Berne 2001 (Cormarë Series 3)

Tolkien in Translation.
> Edited by Thomas Honegger. Zurich and Berne 2003. (Cormarë Series 4)

Mark T. Hooker. *Tolkien Through Russian Eyes*. Zurich and Berne 2003. (Cormarë Series 5)

Forthcoming:

Translating Tolkien.
> Edited by Thomas Honegger. Zurich and Berne 2004. (Cormarë Series 6)

Christopher Garbowski. *Recovery and Transcendence for the Contemporary Mythmaker: The Spiritual Dimension in the Works of J.R.R. Tolkien.* Zurich and Berne 2004 (Cormarë Series 7). Reprint. 1st edition by Marie Curie Sklodowska University Press, Lublin 2000.

Tales of Yore Series

Kay Woollard. *The Terror of Tatty Walk. A Frightener.* CD and Booklet. Zurich and Berne 2000 (Tales of Yore 1)

Kay Woollard, *Wilmot's Very Strange Stone or What came of building "snobbits".* CD and booklet. Zurich and Berne 2001 (Tales of Yore 2)

www.ingramcontent.com/pod-product-compliance
Lightning Source LLC
Chambersburg PA
CBHW050818160426
43192CB00010B/1804